A Stata Companion for the Third Edition of The Fundamentals of Political Science Research

A Stata Companion for the Third Edition of The Fundamentals of Political Science Research offers students a chance to delve into the world of Stata using real political data sets and statistical analysis techniques directly from Paul M. Kellstedt and Guy D. Whitten's best-selling textbook.

Built in parallel with the main text, this workbook teaches students to apply the techniques they learn in each chapter by reproducing the analyses and results from each lesson using Stata. Students will also learn to create all of the tables and figures found in the textbook, leading to an even greater mastery of the core material.

This accessible, informative, and engaging companion walks through the use of Stata step-by-step, using command lines and screenshots to demonstrate proper use of the software. With the help of these guides, students will become comfortable creating, editing, and using data sets in Stata to produce original statistical analyses for evaluating causal claims. End-of-chapter exercises encourage this innovation by asking students to formulate and evaluate their own hypotheses.

Paul M. Kellstedt is Professor of Political Science at Texas A & M University. He is the author of *The Mass Media and the Dynamics of Racial Attitudes* (Cambridge, 2003), winner of Harvard University's John F. Kennedy School of Government's 2004 Goldsmith Book Prize. In addition, he has published numerous articles in a variety of leading journals. He is the Editor-in-chief of *Political Science Research and Methods*, the flagship journal of the European Political Science Association.

Guy D. Whitten is Cullen-McFadden Professor of Political Science, as well as Director of the European Union Center, at Texas A & M University. He has published a variety of articles in leading peer-reviewed journals. He is on the editorial boards of the *American Journal of Political Science, Electoral Studies,* and *Political Science Research and Methods.*

A Stata Companion for the Third Edition of The Fundamentals of Political Science Research

Paul M. Kellstedt
Texas A & M University

Guy D. Whitten
Texas A & M University

CAMBRIDGE
UNIVERSITY PRESS

CAMBRIDGE
UNIVERSITY PRESS

University Printing House, Cambridge CB2 8BS, United Kingdom

One Liberty Plaza, 20th Floor, New York, NY 10006, USA

477 Williamstown Road, Port Melbourne, VIC 3207, Australia

314–321, 3rd Floor, Plot 3, Splendor Forum, Jasola District Centre,
New Delhi – 110025, India

79 Anson Road, #06–04/06, Singapore 079906

Cambridge University Press is part of the University of Cambridge.

It furthers the University's mission by disseminating knowledge in the pursuit of
education, learning, and research at the highest international levels of excellence.

www.cambridge.org
Information on this title: www.cambridge.org/9781108447966
DOI: 10.1017/9781108683791

First published 2020

Printed in the United Kingdom by TJ International Ltd. Padstow Cornwall

A catalogue record for this publication is available from the British Library.

Library of Congress Cataloging-in-Publication Data
Names: Kellstedt, Paul M., 1968– author. | Whitten, Guy D., 1965– author. |
    Kellstedt, Paul M., 1968– Fundamentals of political science research.
Title: A Stata companion for the third edition of the Fundamentals of political
    science research / Paul M. Kellstedt, Guy D. Whitten.
Description: Cambridge, United Kingdom ; New York, NY : Cambridge University
    Press, 2019. | Includes bibliographical references and index.
Identifiers: LCCN 2019011013 | ISBN 9781108447966 (paperback)
Subjects: LCSH: Political science–Research–Handbooks, manuals, etc. |
    Stata–Handbooks, manuals, etc. | Political statistics–Computer
    programs–Handbooks, manuals, etc.
Classification: LCC JA86 .K453 2019 | DDC 320.0285/555–dc23
LC record available at https://lccn.loc.gov/2019011013

ISBN 978-1-108-44796-6 Paperback

Additional resources for this publication at www.cambridge.org/FPSRstata

BRIEF CONTENTS

CONTENTS

PREFACE

We received a wealth of useful feedback from instructors and students about the first two editions of *The Fundamentals of Political Science Research*. In response to feedback on the first edition, we substantially increased the number of end-of-chapter exercises in the second edition. While the response to this increase was positive, we sensed a demand for even more exercises and, in particular, more hands-on material for how to put the techniques that we discuss in the book into action. This workbook is our attempt to meet these demands. It is one of three workbooks, each written to help students to work with the materials covered in the third edition of *The Fundamentals of Political Science Research* using a particular piece of statistical software.

This workbook focuses on using the program Stata. Our expectation is that the modal user of this book will be using a relatively recent version of Stata on a computer that is running some version of the Windows operating system. We also have made an effort to accommodate users who are using some version of macOS or OS X. A webpage available at www.cambridge.org/fpsr will help Mac users with any difficulties.

The chapter structure of this workbook mirrors the chapter structure of the third edition of *The Fundamentals of Political Science Research*. We have written with the expectation that students will read the chapters of this companion after they have read the chapters of the book.

We continue to update both the general and instructor-only sections of the webpage for our book (www.cambridge.org/fpsr). As before, the general section contains data sets available in formats compatible with SPSS, Stata, and R. The instructor-only section contains several additional resources, including PowerPoint and TEX/Beamer slides for each chapter, a test-bank, and answer keys for the exercises.

Paul M. Kellstedt
Guy D. Whitten

FIGURES

1 THE SCIENTIFIC STUDY OF POLITICS

1.1 OVERVIEW

In this chapter we introduce you to some of the important building blocks of a scientific approach to studying politics. As you can already tell from reading the first chapter of the third edition of *The Fundamentals of Political Science Research* – which we will refer to as "*FPSR*" from here on – data are an important part of what we do both to explore the political world and to test hypotheses based on causal theories. An important part of working with data is learning how to use a statistical software package. In the sections that follow, we introduce you to the Stata program and some basics that you will need to get up and running. In doing this, we also introduce some general principles of good computing practices for effectively working with data.

1.2 "A WORKBOOK? WHY IS THERE A WORKBOOK?"

You might be asking yourself this question, and it's perfectly fair to do so. Allow us to try to explain how this workbook fits in with the main *FPSR* text.

As you will see in the weeks and months to follow in your class, the main textbook will teach you about the use of statistics in political science, mostly by using equations and examples. So yes, in some ways, it will feel rather math-y. (And we think that's cool, though we realize that it's not everyone's cup of tea.) One of the ways that people learn about the practice of statistics is to use computer software to calculate statistics directly. To that end, many instructors want students to learn to use a particular computer software package so they can begin to conduct statistical analyses themselves.[1] We have discovered through years of teaching that this transition between equations in a book and software output on a computer screen is a very difficult one. The goal of this software companion book is to make this connection stronger, even seamless.

If we are successful, this book will do two things. First, it will teach the nuts and bolts about how to use Stata. Though many (perhaps most) students today are quite computer-literate, we believe that having a reference guide for students to learn the techniques, or for them to teach themselves out of class time, will be helpful. Second,

---

[1] This particular software companion book teaches students to use Stata, but we have also produced parallel books for instructors who wish to have their students learn SPSS or R.

and more importantly, this software guide will provide explicit hand-holding to you as you learn to connect the key principles from the main text to the practical issues of producing and interpreting statistical results.

Each chapter of this software guide works in parallel with that of the main *FPSR* text. So when you learn the equations of two-variable regression analysis in Chapter 9 of the main text, you will learn the details about using Stata to estimate two-variable regression models in Chapter 9 of this companion book. And so on. In the end, we hope that the very important (but perhaps rather abstract) equations in the text become more meaningful to you as you learn to estimate the statistics yourself, and then learn to interpret them meaningfully and clearly. Those three things – formulae, software, and interpretation – together provide a very solid foundation and basic understanding of social science.

Let's start.

1.3   GETTING STARTED WITH STATA

To get started with Stata, we recommend that you set yourself up in front of a computer that has the program installed with a copy of *FPSR* close by. You should also have the set of computer files that accompany this text (which you can download from the text's web site, www.cambridge.org/fpsr) in a directory on the computer on which you are working. You will get the most out of this workbook by working in Stata as you read this workbook.

The instructions in this book can help you learn Stata whether you use a Windows-based PC or a Mac. Once the program is launched, Stata works identically, no matter which platform you use. Mac users should be aware, though, that our screenshots will come from a Windows-based PC. Some of those screenshots that involve finding and opening files on your computer, therefore, will look somewhat unfamiliar to Mac users, but we assume that Mac users are at least somewhat used to this. Overall, the differences between running Stata on Windows compared to a Mac are minimal. That said, we have created a help guide on the differences between working with Stata on a Windows-based PC and a Mac operating system, which can be found online at www.cambridge.org/fpsr.

Finally, we wrote this book while using versions 14 and 15 of Stata. Particularly for the statistical fundamentals you will learn in this book, the differences between versions – at least as old as Stata 12 – are not severe. In fact, if you use any version of Stata between 12 and 15, you might not notice the difference between what appears on your screen and what appears in the screenshots contained in this book.

1.3.1   Launching Stata

When you are sitting in front of a computer on which Stata has been properly installed, you can launch the program by double-clicking on the Stata icon or by finding the Stata program on your start menu. Once you have successfully launched the Stata program,

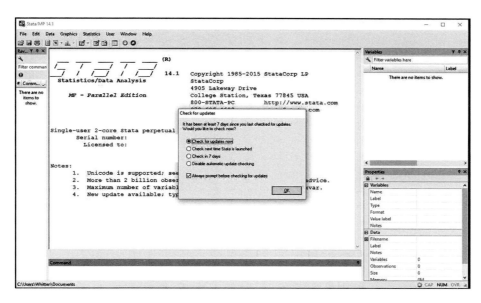

Figure 1.1: Stata after initial launch with update options box

you will sometimes be prompted with a small box of options for updating the program like what we see in Figure 1.1. If this box does pop up when you launch the program, then we recommend that, for now, you click the option "Check next time Stata is launched" and then click "OK."

At this point, you should see one large window like that in Figure 1.2. Within this main Stata window, you will see four other windows labeled "Review" (on the left side), "Variables" (on the top right side), "Properties" (on the bottom right side), and "Command" (across the bottom). The remaining area in the middle, known as the "Results" window, is not labeled. If you are seeing all of this, you are ready to go.

1.3.2   Getting Stata to Do Things

In almost any mainstream statistical program today, there are multiple ways to accomplish the same tasks. In Stata, almost any command can be executed using pull-down menus, typed commands in the command window, or typed commands in a do-file window. The choice of which of these options to use is a matter of personal comfort. But, as we discuss below, no matter which way you choose to get Stata to do things, you need to keep track of what you are doing. We now discuss the three ways to get Stata to do things by showing an example of opening a data set. We recommend that you try all three, but especially the example of using a do-file in Section 1.3.2.

Using Pull-down Menus

If you prefer to use pull-down menus, you need to start with either the row of textual headings across the top left of the program (starting with "File," then "Edit," etc.) or,

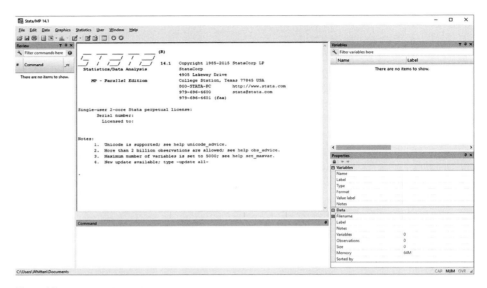

Figure 1.2: Stata initial launch

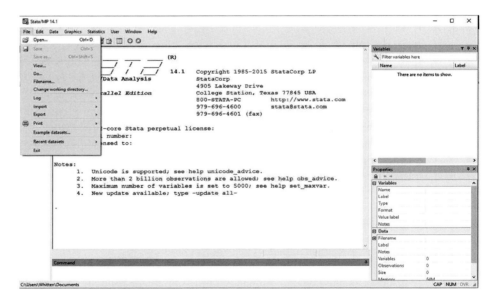

Figure 1.3: Stata with pull-down menu for "File" selected

immediately under that, the row of icons (a picture of a folder opening, a picture of a floppy disk, etc.). In our initial example, we are going to open a data set, so we need to start with either the textual heading "File" or the icon that looks like a folder being opened. In Figure 1.3, we show what this will look like if you click on "File."

Once you have clicked on "File," you will want to direct Stata to the location on your computer where you have placed the *FPSR* Stata companion files (as we noted above,

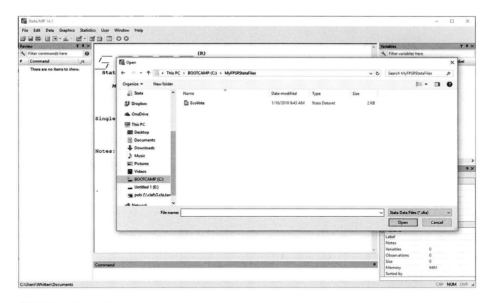

Figure 1.4: Stata with directory open

these can be downloaded from www.cambridge.org/fpsr). In our running example, these files are located in the directory "C:\MyFPSRStataFiles." So, to find our initial data set, named "EcoVote," we would point Stata to this directory and then click on the file "EcoVote" as shown in Figure 1.4.

Once you have done this correctly, your Stata screen should look like Figure 1.5. A few things have changed:

- In the "Results" window we can see the text
  `. use "C:\MyFPSRStataFiles\EcoVote.dta", clear`
  where

  - the "`.`" in front of this line indicates that this is a command that Stata has executed,
  - the name of the command is "`use`" which is the main Stata command for accessing a data set,
  - the text in double quotes tells us the location where the file was obtained, and
  - the "`, clear`" tells us that Stata cleared out any data that we had sitting in the program's memory before it opened our data set.

- In the upper left corner, at the top of the "Review" window, we see the number 1 in the "#" column followed by the beginning of the text of the command. This is where Stata keeps track of each command that it has executed.

- On the right side, we can see that there is new information in the "Variables" and "Properties" windows:

Figure 1.5: Stata with data loaded in

- From the "Variables" window, we can see the names of the three variables that are contained in this data set.
- From the "Properties" window we can see some information about each variable and some information about the data set. In particular, we can tell that the data set contains 3 variables, 36 observations, and takes up 64 megabytes of memory.

Using the Command Window

You can type commands directly into the command window that you see across the bottom of the initial window that opens when you launch the program. These commands are typed in one at a time and are executed by the program when you hit the "Enter" button on your keyboard.

So, if we want to load the data set "EcoVote" which is a Stata data set (with the ".dta" suffix), you would type the following command into the "Command" window and hit the "Enter" key on your computer:

```
use "C:\MyFPSRStataFiles\EcoVote.dta", clear
```

If you have done this correctly, your Stata will look like Figure 1.5. [2]

---

[2] The location of files is often a stumbling block for beginning users of a statistical software package. To keep things simple, we recommend that you create a folder on your computer's C drive named "MyFPSRStataFiles" and put all of the files that you have downloaded from www.cambridge.org/fpsr into that folder. If you are unable to do this, then on a computer using a Windows operating system you can find the exact name of the location of a file by right-clicking on that file, left-clicking "Properties" and then looking at the entry to the right of "Location." This filepath, or location, can be selected, copied and pasted directly into your command window (or do-file) to insure that it is exactly right. As discussed

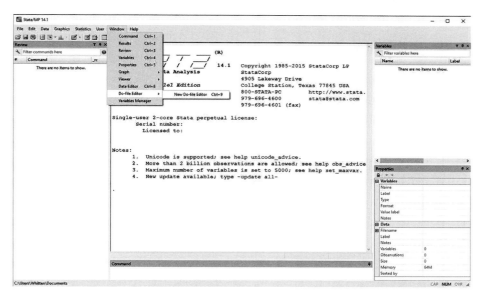

Figure 1.6: Opening a new do-file window

Using a Do-file

A third way to issue commands in Stata is to use a do-file. While this method of working will seem a little bit clumsy at first, it is our preferred method of working in Stata for reasons that we will explain below. To work with a do-file, you need to open a new window called a "Do-file Editor." To do this, go to the pull-down menus on the top left of the program and select "Window," "Do-file Editor," and finally left-click on "New Do-file Editor," as shown in Figure 1.6. We will eventually cover a lot of different things that one can do with a do-file, but for now, all that we want you to do is to type the following command into the new do-file:

```
use "C:\MyFPSRStataFiles\EcoVote.dta", clear
```

Once you have typed this command into the do-file editor, you will then want to select the entire line – you can do this by left-clicking at the beginning of the line and then moving to the end and releasing the left mouse button – and then click on the icon at the right side of the top of the do-file window that looks like a piece of paper with writing on it with an arrow pointing to the right in the lower right corner of the icon. Clicking on this icon, named "Execute Selection (do)," will tell the program to execute the selected line of code. In Figure 1.7, we show what this will look like right before you click on "Execute Selection (do)." Once you have done this correctly, you will see output in the main window that looks like Figure 1.5.

earlier, a help guide on the differences between working on a Windows-based PC and a Mac operating system can be found online at www.cambridge.org/fpsr.

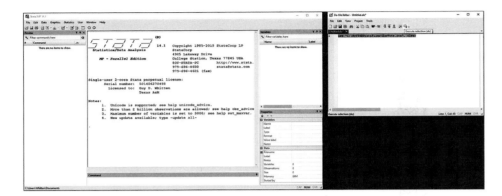

Figure 1.7: Executing a command from a do-file editor

1.3.3   Initially Examining Data in Stata

Now that we have shown you three different ways to get a data set into Stata, we want you to take a look at the data that you have loaded into the program.[3] These data are from a famous study of economic voting conducted by Ray Fair (Fair 1978). They contain values of economic growth and incumbent party vote from US Presidential elections between 1876 and 2016. To get an initial look at these data, click on the "Data Editor (Browse)" icon which can be found in the top left of the main Stata window – it is the icon that looks like a spreadsheet with a magnifying glass over it. Once you have done this, your computer should look something like Figure 1.8. Each column in this spreadsheet contains values for a single variable and each row contains data from a single election. You are now ready to proceed to the end-of-chapter exercises.

1.4   EXERCISES

1. Go through all of the steps described above. Once you have the "Data Editor (Browse)" open (so that your computer looks like Figure 1.8), do the following:
    (a) Look at the values in the column labeled "growth." This is Fair's measure of percentage change in real GDP per capita. Do the following:
        i.   Identify the year with the highest value for this variable.
        ii.   Identify the year with the lowest value for this variable.
        iii. What does it mean if this variable goes up by 1?
    (b) Look at the values in the column labeled "inc_vote." This is Fair's measure of the percentage of major party votes cast for the party of the president at the time of the election. Now do the following:
        i.   Identify the year with the highest value for this variable.
        ii.   Identify the year with the lowest value for this variable.
        iii. What does it mean if this variable goes up by 1?

---

[3] We discuss how to manually enter your own data into a Stata file in a webpage, available at www.cambridge.org/fpsr.

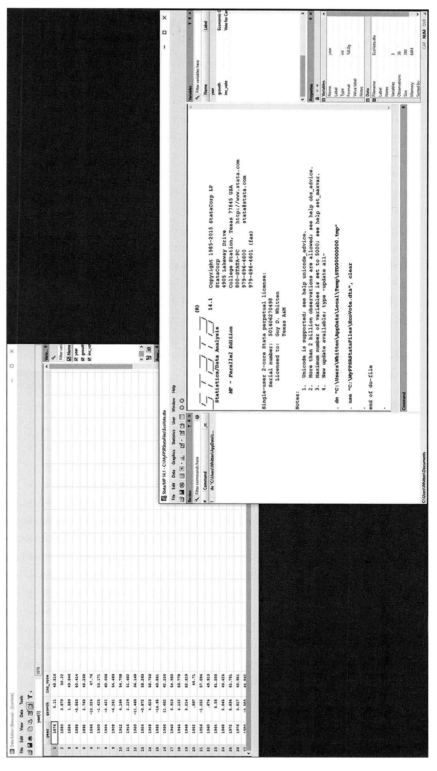

Figure 1.8. Initially examining data in Stata

2 THE ART OF THEORY BUILDING

2.1 OVERVIEW

One of our emphases in the book has been on producing new causal theories, and then evaluating whether or not those theories are supported by evidence. In this chapter, we describe how to explore sources of variation – both across space, and across time – to get you started thinking about new explanations for interesting phenomena. We also help you explore how new theories can be built upon the existing work in the literature.

2.2 EXAMINING VARIATION ACROSS TIME AND ACROSS SPACE

As we discuss in Section 2.3 of *FPSR*, one way to develop ideas about causal theories is to identify interesting variation. In that section, we discuss examining two types of variation, cross-sectional and time-series variation. In this section, we show you how to create figures like the ones presented in Section 2.3 of *FPSR*. Although there are many different types of graphs that can be used to examine variation in variables, we recommend a bar graph for cross-sectional variation and a connected plot for time-series variation.

As you will see from these examples, Stata's graph commands can often be quite long because of all of the options that we typically like to include. We therefore recommend that you start with the main command and then add the options until you get a figure that looks right to you. For the example of the bar graph, we go through these steps in some detail.

2.2.1 Producing a Bar Graph for Examining Cross-Section Variation

A useful way to get a sense of the variation for a cross-sectional variable is to produce a bar graph in which you display the values of that variable across spatial units. In the example that we display in Figure 2.1 of *FPSR*, we have a bar graph of military spending as a percentage of gross domestic product in 2005 for 22 randomly selected nations. Building on what we learned in Chapter 1, we will now show you how to produce a figure like this in Stata. The first step to doing this is the command:

```
use "C:\MyFPSRStataFiles\milspend_pct_05.dta", clear
```

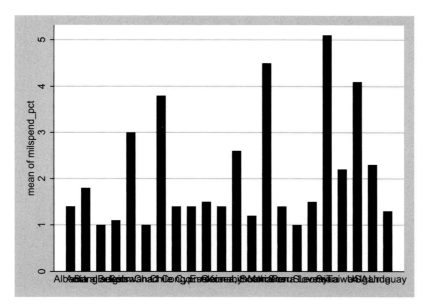

Figure 2.1: Initial bar graph of military spending

which will load the appropriate data set into Stata. Once you have this data set properly loaded into Stata, you will want to issue a command to produce a bar graph of the variable "`milspend_pct`" for each spatial unit. In this case, the spatial unit is `nation`. So the command for producing such a bar graph is:

```
graph bar milspend_pct, over(nation)
```

where "`graph bar`" tells Stata that we want to produce a bar graph. The next part of the command, "`milspend_pct`," is the name of the variable whose values we want to graph. By default, commands in Stata are written on a single line and submitted to the program. We can break each command into the main part of the command and then the optional part of the command. The optional part is the text that follows a comma. So, for this command the option that we have chosen with ", `over(nation)`" tells the program that we want to have a bar graph across the values of "`nation`." We can see the results from submitting this command in Figure 2.1. Although we have the values of "`milspend_pct`" displayed in a bar graph, we are unable to read names of the nations for which these values are displayed. This is because they have all been displayed horizontally under each bar and they run into each other. To fix this, we can add a further option to our command by typing:

```
graph bar milspend_pct, over(nation, label(angle(45)))
```

where ", `label(angle(45))`" tells Stata that we want the labels displayed at a 45 degree angle. The result from this command is displayed in Figure 2.2.

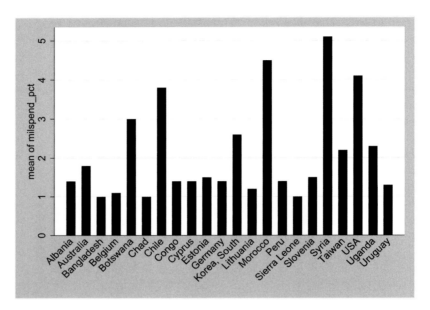

Figure 2.2: Initial bar graph of military spending with angled labels

Compare Figure 2.2 with Figure 2.1 in *FPSR*. What is the difference between these two figures? The answer is that in Figure 2.1 in *FPSR* the values of military spending have been sorted from smallest to largest. When displaying data in graphs, it is important that you do so in a fashion that allows you and your readers to most easily make the assessments that they want to make. In this case, since we are trying to think about what makes a country spend more or less of its GDP on its military, we want to be able to see which countries spend more or less. Try comparing the value of military spending between Belgium and Lithuania in the graph that we just made, Figure 2.2. Not an easy thing to do! It's a lot easier using Figure 2.1 from *FPSR* because the cases have been *sorted*. You might have also noticed that the label on the vertical axis in Figure 2.1 of *FPSR* is more communicative. We can make these two adjustments by writing the command:

```
graph bar milspend_pct, /*
*/ , over(nation, label(angle(45)) sort( milspend_pct)) /*
*/ scheme(s1mono) /*
*/ ytitle("Military Expenditures as a Percentage of GDP")
```

where "sort(milspend_pct)" tells Stata to sort the bars by the values of "milspend_pct" and "ytitle("Military Expenditures as a Percentage of GDP")" tells Stata to insert a more informative label on the *y* axis. There are two additional elements of this command that need to be explained. First, you will have probably noticed that this command now takes up four lines, with each line except for the first started with a "/*" and each line except for the last ended with a "*/." We have done this because Stata reads each line as a new command. When Stata encounters a "/*," it ignores everything until it sees a "*/." Thus Stata reads the four lines of code that we have written above as though they were strung together as one single line of code. One alternative would be for us to have written all four lines above as one single long line. But the problem with this alternative is that it would be difficult for us to keep track of. And, second, you will probably have noticed the option "scheme(s1mono)" on the third line of this command. This tells Stata that we want the graph to be drawn using the graphics scheme named "s1mono." The different graphics schemes in Stata determine the overall look of the figures that Stata produces. You can find out more about these by issuing the command "help graph scheme" and then left-clicking on the blue text "schemes intro."

All of the commands for this example are contained in a do-file called "Chapter 2 Bar Graph Example.do" which can be found in the MyFPSRStataFiles directory.

2.2.2 Producing a Connected Plot for Examining Time-Series Variation

A useful way to get a sense of the variation for a time-series variable is to produce a connected plot in which you display the values of that variable *connected* across time. In the example that we display in Figure 2.2 of *FPSR*, we have a connected plot of the values for presidential approval each month from February 1995 to December 2005. Building on what we learned in Chapter 1, we will now show you how to produce a figure like this in Stata. As with the previous example, the first step to doing this is to run the command:

```
use "C:\MyFPSRStataFiles\presap9505.dta", clear
```

which loads the data. The command for producing Figure 2.2 of *FPSR* is:

```
graph twoway connected presap year_month , /*
*/ xlabel(420(6)540, angle(45)) ytitle("Presidential Approval") /*
*/ xtitle("Year/Month") legend(off) scheme(s1mono)
```

where

- "graph twoway connected" tells Stata that we want to produce a graph from the "twoway" set of graphs[1] and that the specific type of twoway graph that we want is a "connected" graph,[2]
- "presap" and "year-month" are the variables that will define the vertical and horizontal dimensions of the graph,
- the comma after "year-month" indicates the start of the options part of the command,

---

[1] As we will see in later chapters, Stata has a large number of different twoway graphs.

[2] A connected graph is one in which a circle represents each observation and then these circles are connected together by lines.

- "`xlabel(420(6)540, angle(45))`" tells Stata that we want to label the time points from time point 420 to 540 with labels every 6 points[3] and that, as we did in the previous section, we want labels to appear at a 45 degree angle,
- "`ytitle("Presidential Approval")`" and "`xtitle("Year/Month")`" tell Stata the variable labels for the vertical and horizontal axes,
- "`legend(off)`" tells Stata that we do not want a legend box to appear at the bottom of our graph, and
- "`scheme(s1mono)`" tells Stata that we want the graph to be produced using the scheme "s1mono."

In Chapter 12, we will introduce you to a series of commands associated with time-series data and some other ways in which to produce graphs of time-series data. All of the commands for this example are contained in a do-file called "Chapter 2 Connected Graph Example.do" which can be found in the MyFPSRStataFiles directory.

2.3   USING GOOGLE SCHOLAR TO SEARCH THE LITERATURE EFFECTIVELY

We assume that you're skilled at web searches, likely using Google's search engine. In addition to the myriad other things that Google allows us to search for on the internet, it has a dedicated search engine for scholarly publications like books and journal articles. The aspects of Google you're likely most familiar with come from Google's home page – www.google.com. The searches that they enable through scholarly work, however, using what they call "Google Scholar," is at a different site: https://scholar.google.com. That site looks a good bit like Google's home page, but when you're at Google Scholar, it's searching a different corner of the internet entirely – the part where academic journals and books are uploaded.

Figure 2.3 shows the Google Scholar home page. If you have a Google account (like a Gmail address), you can save items in "My Library" – we'll show you how to do that shortly – that you can access any time. The articles are normally saved as an Adobe .PDF file. You'll notice the familiar search box that looks like Google's normal home page. You can tell from the figure, though, that despite the similarities in appearances, this web site is https://scholar.google.com.

So let's see how Google Scholar works. In the first chapter of *FPSR*, we introduced you to what we called the theory of economic voting. The seminal article in the study of economic voting was conducted by an economist named Ray Fair. So let's see what happens when we type "Ray Fair economic voting" in the Google Scholar search bar.

Figure 2.4 shows the results of that Google Scholar search. As luck would have it, the first search result happens to be that path-breaking article. Let's examine that result. If

---

[3] As we discuss in Chapter 12, Stata has a particular way of dealing with time-series data. Time-series dates are given unique identifying values. In the case of Stata's conventions for dealing with monthly data, such as those in this example, January 1960 is assigned the unique identifying value of 0. This means that January 1995 is assigned the value 420 and December 540. Although our data begin in February of 1995, we decided to start the display of the months on the horizontal dimension of Figure 2.2 in *FPSR* in January 1995.

Figure 2.3: The Google Scholar home page

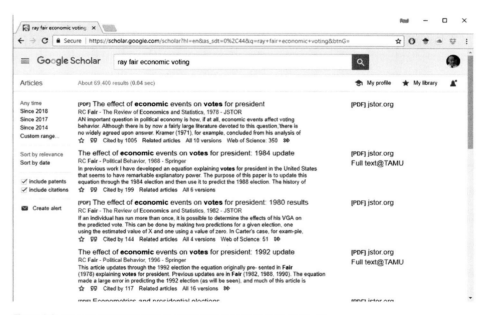

Figure 2.4: Google Scholar results for "Ray Fair economic voting" search

you look to the far right of the selection, you see the text "[PDF] jstor.org," which shows you what format the file is available in – in this case, an Adobe .PDF – and where – in this case, at the archive www.jstor.org. Your college or university's library almost surely has a subscription to JStor that your student fees pay for, and so if you're on a campus internet connection (as opposed to a Wi-Fi network at your home, or on a cellular network), clicking on "[PDF] jstor.org" will take you to the article. (If you're on your home Wi-Fi network, then JStor doesn't know that you're a university student, and the publisher might ask you to pay a rather steep fee for access to the article. So beware about where you can do these searches for free.)

There's a lot of other information that the Google Scholar search reveals, though. First, if you want to save the Ray Fair article to your "My Library," then click on the ★ at the lower left of the item, and you'll be able to access that .PDF anywhere.

Importantly, you can also see how influential every article has been to date. In Figure 2.4, you can see text near the bottom of the citation that says "Cited by 1005" – which means that the Fair article has been cited 1005 times to date.[4] That number indicates that the paper has been massively influential.[5]

Of course, that doesn't necessarily mean that 1005 other articles all cite the Fair article approvingly. Some might; others might not. But being agreed with, or being "proved right," isn't the highest value in science. It's far better to be an influential part of an ongoing debate while being proved wrong in some respects, than it is to be indisputably correct but ignored by other scholars.

Perhaps you say to yourself, "Sure, Professor Fair wrote an influential article on economic voting a good long while before I was born. What kind of work is being done on the topic *now*?" This is one of the places where Google Scholar is fabulous. That "Cited by 1005" is clickable. You can literally see the list of all 1005 articles that cite the Fair article if you want. (Of course, it would take you a while to sift through them!)

Figure 2.5 shows the results when you click the "Cited by 1005," and then click the "Since 2017" option on the left side of the screen. (You can pick "since" any year you like, obviously.) Just beneath the search bar in Figure 2.5, you'll see the text in light gray saying "About 28 results," indicating that, since 2017, the Fair article has been cited by 28 other articles. So it continues to have influence today.

This is a good way to start the process of exploring a particular topic in academic writing that interests you. This example began by having us tell you that the initial article that spawned all of this interest was written by Ray Fair. So we incorporated his name, obviously, into the search terms. Often, to be sure, this isn't the case.

Just like with using any internet search engine, there's something of a skill in figuring out how to efficiently search for the material you want without getting bogged down with lots of results that aren't interesting to you. Should you use quotation marks in your search, or in a portion of your search terms? Sometimes yes, sometimes no. (In the example above, we did not.) As a general rule, it might be best to try it both ways to see if you get different results.

We have not exhausted all there is to know about how to use Google Scholar here, of course. For example, many scholars have created "Google Scholar profiles," which

---

[4] If you conduct that same search today, the number would surely be higher; our search was conducted on January 9, 2018. Citations tend to accumulate over time.

[5] Of course, you should be careful to remember the original publication date when interpreting citation counts as a measure of impact. Fair's article was published in 1978, so it's not as if some scholars who work in this area have somehow not yet heard of his article. But for an article published more recently – say in 2016 – its impact cannot yet fully be known. That merely means that we don't yet know if the article is likely to have a large impact. Only time will tell.

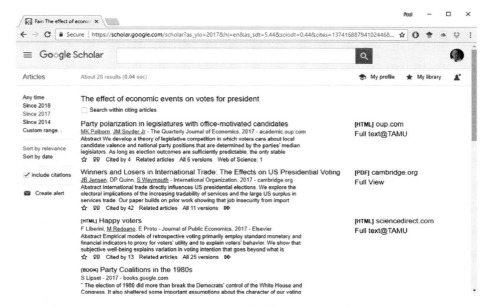

Figure 2.5: Google Scholar search results of articles citing Ray Fair (1978) article

enable you to see the list of scholarly articles and books that they have authored, usually sorted from those with the most citations to the ones with the least. This can help you find similar articles, too, because many scholars work on a topic over the course of many years, and therefore their earlier articles are related to their more recent ones. In Figure 2.5, for example, you can see the scholars whose names are underlined; those are clickable links to those scholars' respective Google Scholar profiles. In addition, the "Help" section of Google Scholar is surprisingly helpful![6]

2.4   WRAPPING UP

In the main text, we discussed how important it is that our theories be new and original – that is, that we aren't merely repeating the ideas and claims of previous scholars. One of the important preconditions for doing something genuinely new is to be familiar with the works that have already been produced on that same topic. Having the vast archive of journal articles and even many books available online – and freely accessible, thanks to your university's libraries – through storage sites like www.jstor.org has been the first step in making this task a lot easier than it was in decades past. The second step has been the invention of very sophisticated search engines like Google Scholar to help us find the previous studies that we otherwise might have missed.

---

[6] In light gray text, you can see the "Help" link that you can click in the bottom-right of Figure 2.3.

2.5   EXERCISES

1. Conduct a search for the following terms using both Google's home page (www.google.com) and Google Scholar (https://scholar.google.com). Only include the quotation marks in your search if we include them. Report the similarities and differences you observe in the first page of the search results:
    (a) "presidential approval"
    (b) "nuclear proliferation"
    (c) nuclear proliferation

2. Open Stata and load the do-file named "Chapter 2 Bar Graph Example.do" into the do-file editor. Make sure that you have the correct directory path for loading the data. In other words, if "C:\MyFPSRStataFiles" is not where you have your data, change this part of the do-file so that the data load into Stata.
    (a) Once you have done this, run the code to produce the graph presented in Figure 2.1 from *FPSR*. Open a word processing document and then copy the figure from Stata and paste it into your word processing document.
    (b) Write a short summary of what you see in this figure.

3. Open Stata and load the do-file named "Chapter 2 Connected Graph Example.do" into the do-file editor. Make sure that you have the correct directory path for loading the data. In other words, if "C:\MyFPSRStataFiles" is not where you have your data, change this part of the do-file so that the data load into Stata.
    (a) Once you have done this, run the code to produce the graph presented in Figure 2.2 from *FPSR*. Open a word processing document and then copy the figure from Stata and paste it into your word processing document.
    (b) Write a short summary of what you see in this figure.

3 EVALUATING CAUSAL RELATIONSHIPS

3.1 OVERVIEW

Unlike the previous two chapters, in Chapters 3 through 5, there will not be any computer-based lessons in Stata or elsewhere. Not to worry, though. There will be more than enough time for intensive computer work later in the book. We promise!

In this abbreviated chapter, then, we offer some expanded exercises that will apply the lessons learned in the main text, and build on the skills from the first two chapters.

3.2 EXERCISES

1. Causal claims are common in media stories about news and politics. Sometimes they are explicitly stated, but often they are implicit. For each of the following news stories, identify the key causal claim in the story, and whether, based on the information given, you are convinced that all four causal hurdles have been crossed. (But remember that most media stories aren't the original generators of causal claims; they merely report on the news as they see fit to do so.)

   (a) www.cnn.com/2018/01/16/politics/freedom-house-democracy-trump-report/index.html

   (b) https://thehill.com/opinion/energy-environment/368355-wheres-the-proof-climate-change-causes-the-polar-vortex

   (c) www.foxnews.com/us/california-mudslides-where-and-why-they-happen

   (d) www.aljazeera.com/news/2018/01/trump-muslim-ban-shifted-public-opinion-study-finds-180113092728118.html

   (e) www.npr.org/player/embed/575959966/576606076 (Podcast)

2. Candidates for public office make causal claims all the time. For each of the following snippets from a key speech made by a candidate, identify the key causal claim made in the speech, and whether, based on the information given, you are convinced that all four causal hurdles have been crossed. (But remember that candidates for office are not scientists responsible for testing causal claims; they are trying to persuade voters to support them over their opponent.)

   (a) "America is one of the highest-taxed nations in the world. Reducing taxes will cause new companies and new jobs to come roaring back into our country. Then we are going to deal with the issue of regulation, one of the greatest job-killers of them all. Excessive regulation is costing our country as much as $2 trillion a year, and we will end it. We are going to lift the restrictions on the production of American energy. This will produce more than $20 trillion in job-creating economic activity over the next four decades." (Excerpt from Donald Trump's speech accepting the Republican nomination for President, July 21, 2016.)

(b)   "Now, I don't think President Obama and Vice President Biden get the credit they deserve for saving us from the worst economic crisis of our lifetimes. Our economy is so much stronger than when they took office. Nearly 15 million new private-sector jobs. Twenty million more Americans with health insurance. And an auto industry that just had its best year ever. That's real progress." (Excerpt from Hillary Clinton's speech accepting the Democratic nomination for President, July 28, 2016.)

(c)   "The truth is, on issue after issue that would make a difference in your lives – on health care and education and the economy – Sen. McCain has been anything but independent. He said that our economy has made 'great progress' under this president. He said that the fundamentals of the economy are strong. And when one of his chief advisers – the man who wrote his economic plan – was talking about the anxiety Americans are feeling, he said that we were just suffering from a 'mental recession,' and that we've become, and I quote, 'a nation of whiners.'" (Excerpt from Barack Obama's speech accepting the Democratic nomination for President, August 28, 2008.)

(d)   "His [Barack Obama's] policies have not helped create jobs, they have depressed them. And this I can tell you about where President Obama would take America: His plan to raise taxes on small business won't add jobs, it will eliminate them; … And his trillion-dollar deficits will slow our economy, restrain employment, and cause wages to stall." (Excerpt from Mitt Romney's speech accepting the Republican nomination for President, August 30, 2012.)

3.   Political science, as we have argued, revolves around the making and evaluation of causal claims. Find each of the following research articles – Google Scholar makes it easy to do so – and then identify the key causal claim made in the article. Then produce a causal hurdles scorecard, and decide to what degree you are convinced that all four causal hurdles have been crossed. Some of the statistical material presented in the articles will, this early in the semester, be beyond your comprehension. That will change as the semester rolls along! (And remember that political scientists are trained to be experts in testing causal claims. So set the bar high.)

(a)   Heberlig, E., Hetherington, M. and Larson, B. 2006. "The price of leadership: Campaign money and the polarization of congressional parties." *Journal of Politics* 68(4): 992–1005.

(b) Stasavage, D. 2005. "Democracy and education spending in Africa." *American Journal of Political Science* 49(2): 343–358.

(c) De Mesquita, B.B., Morrow, J.D., Siverson, R.M. and Smith, A. 1999. "An institutional explanation of the democratic peace." *American Political Science Review* 93(4): 791–807.

(d) Lipsmeyer, C.S. and Pierce, H.N. 2011. "The eyes that bind: Junior ministers as oversight mechanisms in coalition governments." *Journal of Politics* 73(4): 1152–1164.

4 RESEARCH DESIGN

4.1 OVERVIEW

As was the case in Chapter 3, there will not be any computer-based lessons in Stata or elsewhere. Again, we offer some expanded exercises that will apply the lessons learned in the main text.

4.2 EXERCISES

1. Recall from the main text (Section 4.2.4) that one of the drawbacks to conducting experiments is that not all X variables are subject to experimental control and random assignment. And so there are a lot of substantive problems in political science that we might *wish* to study experimentally, but which might seem to be impossible to study with experimental methods. Imagine the following causal questions, and write a paragraph about what would be required to conduct an experiment in that particular research situation, being careful to refer to both halves of the two-part definition of an experiment in your answer. (Warning: Some of them will seem impossible, or nearly impossible, or might require time travel.)

   (a) Does the development of state-sponsored universities cause economic development to rise?

   (b) Has the establishment of independent central banks to control monetary policy caused a reduction in the severity of recessions?

   (c) Does an individual's religiosity cause a person's level of opposition to same-sex marriage?

   (d) Does a country's openness to trade cause blue-collar workers' wages to fall?

   (e) Does having a more professionalized legislature cause states to respond more quickly to voters' preferences?

   (f) Does having a more racially diverse set of school administrators and teachers cause a reduction in student suspensions and expulsions?

2. For each of the above research situations, if you were *unable* to perform an experiment, name at least one Z variable that could potentially confound the X–Y

relationship, and would need to be controlled for in some other manner, in an observational study.

3. Assuming that you were unable to conduct an experiment for the aforementioned research situations, describe an observational study that you might conduct instead. In each case, is the study you envision a cross-sectional or time-series observational study? Why?

4. Consider the following research question: Does exposure to stories in the news media shape an individual's policy opinions?

    (a) Write a short paragraph trying to explain the causal mechanism that might be at work here.

    (b) If we wanted to study this relationship using an experiment, what would the barriers to conducting the experiment be?

    (c) What, if any, are the ethical considerations involved in studying that relationship experimentally?

    (d) What are the benefits of exploring that relationship experimentally? In other words, what specific Z variables would be controlled for in an experiment that could potentially be confounding in an observational study?

    (e) Read the following article and write a one-paragraph summary of it:

    - King, G., Schneer, B. and White, A. 2017. "How the news media activate public expression and influence national agendas." *Science* 358(6364): 776–780.

5. Consider the relationship between the level of democracy in a country and the country's respect for human rights.

    (a) Describe both a cross-sectional and a time-series observational design that would help test the theory that increase in the level of democracy causes a country to increase its respect for human rights.

    (b) What concerns would you have about crossing the four causal hurdles in each case?

6. Using the model described in Section 4.4 of the main text, write a one-paragraph summary of the following research articles:

    (a) Stasavage, D. 2005. "Democracy and education spending in Africa." *American Journal of Political Science* 49(2): 343–358.

    (b) O'Brien, D.Z. 2015. "Rising to the top: Gender, political performance, and party leadership in parliamentary democracies." *American Journal of Political Science* 59(4): 1022–1039.

    (c) Fortunato, D., Stevenson, R.T. and Vonnahme, G. 2016. "Context and political knowledge: Explaining cross-national variation in partisan left–right knowledge." *Journal of Politics* 78(4): 1211–1228.

    (d) Titiunik, R. 2016. "Drawing your senator from a jar: Term length and legislative behavior." *Political Science Research and Methods* 4(2): 293–316.

    (e) Bansak, K., Hainmueller, J. and Hangartner, D. 2016. "How economic, humanitarian, and religious concerns shape European attitudes toward asylum seekers." *Science* 354(6309): aag2147.

5 MEASURING CONCEPTS OF INTEREST

5.1   OVERVIEW

As was the case in Chapters 3 and 4, there will not be any computer-based lessons in Stata or elsewhere. Again, we offer some expanded exercises that will apply the lessons learned in the main text.

5.2   EXERCISES

1. Consider, for a moment, the concept of "customer satisfaction." For now, let's define it as "the degree to which a product or service meets or exceeds a customer's expectations." So, like other concepts, it is a variable: Some customers are very satisfied, some have mixed experiences, and some are very unhappy. Companies – and even some government agencies – are interested for obvious reasons in understanding that variation. Now answer the following questions:

    (a) How well do you think Yelp reviews serve as a measure of customer satisfaction? Explain your answer.

    (b) Read "The Happiness Button" in the February 5, 2018, issue of *The New Yorker*: www.newyorker.com/magazine/2018/02/05/customer-satisfaction-at-the-push-of-a-button. What are the strengths and weaknesses of the strategy pursued by HappyOrNot in terms of measuring the concept of customer satisfaction?

    (c) The article describes the push button measures of satisfaction at security checkpoints in London's Heathrow Airport. What are the strengths and weaknesses of such an approach? If, on a particular day, there was a higher share of "frown" responses, what would that tell (and what wouldn't that tell) to the officials at Heathrow?

2. The concept of "political knowledge" is a very important one in the study of public opinion and political behavior, as it lies at the heart of many influential theories of why citizens hold the opinions that they do, and why they vote the way that they do. Answer the following questions:

    (a) Conceptually, how would you define political knowledge? Try to be as specific as possible.

(b) Measuring political knowledge, as you might imagine, can be a bit tricky. For years, the American National Election Studies (ANES) measured the concept by asking a small list of factual questions about politics. The questions were of the form:

> "Now we have a set of questions concerning various public figures. We want to see how much information about them gets out to the public from television, newspapers and the like... [NAME] – What job or political office does he [or she] NOW hold?"

Survey respondents were not given a closed-ended list of response options from which to choose; instead, they were allowed to respond freely, and their responses were recorded verbatim. After the survey was completed, coders would look at the response transcript and judge whether the answers were correct or not. A respondent's score on the political knowledge scale, then, would be the sum total of the number of correct answers given. What are the various strengths and weaknesses of such an approach?

(c) Skim the following article, which pertains to these types of survey questions: www.jstor.org/stable/pdf/24572671.pdf. What are the main problems identified with the survey items? What effects did these problems have on measuring political knowledge?

(d) In more recent surveys, the ANES has been asking different types of survey questions to measure political knowledge. These questions are closed-ended, and for most, respondents are given a fixed list of options from which to choose. Here are two examples from the 2012 survey:

> "On which of the following does the U.S. federal government currently spend the least?" [Response options (in random order): Foreign aid; Medicare; National defense; Social security.]

> "For how many years is a United States Senator elected – that is, how many years are there in one full term of office for a U.S. Senator?" [No response options given; exact number recorded.]

What are the potential strengths and weaknesses of this revised strategy to measure political knowledge?

(e) Can you think of an alternative measurement strategy for this concept?

3. The concept of "consumer confidence" is important in the study of economics and political science, among other disciplines.

(a) Go to https://news.google.com and search for "consumer confidence" (and be sure to use the quotation marks). From the search results, pick a recent news article that discusses consumer confidence. (Print out the article and include it with your homework.) How well, if at all, does the article define consumer confidence, or how it is measured?

(b) From what you know, offer a conceptual definition of consumer confidence.

(c) There are two major surveys in the US that measure consumer confidence on monthly intervals. One of them is the Survey of Consumers at the University of Michigan. They produce what they call an Index of Consumer Sentiment, which is composed of responses to five survey items. One of the five is as follows:

> "Looking ahead, which would you say is more likely – that in the country as a whole we'll have continuous good times during the next five years or so, or that we will have periods of widespread unemployment or depression, or what?"

What are the potential strengths and weaknesses of this survey question as one component of consumer confidence?

(d) All five of the items in the Michigan Index of Consumer Sentiment can be found here: https://data.sca.isr.umich.edu/fetchdoc.php?docid=24770. How are the five items similar to one another, and how are they different from one another?

(e) The complete monthly survey can be found here: https://data.sca.isr.umich.edu/fetchdoc.php?docid=24776. You will note that the survey does not contain *any* questions to measure a survey respondent's political beliefs or affiliations. Why do you think that is the case?

(f) Can you think of any additional survey questions that might complement or replace the ones in the Michigan Index?

6 GETTING TO KNOW YOUR DATA

6.1 OVERVIEW

In this chapter we introduce you to the commands needed to produce descriptive statistics and graphs using Stata. If you're feeling a little rusty on the basics of Stata that we covered in Chapters 1 and 2, it would be good to review them before diving into this chapter.

In Chapter 6 of *FPSR* we discussed a variety of tools that can be used to get to know your data one variable at a time. In this chapter, we discuss how to produce output in Stata to allow you to get to know your variables. An important first step to getting to know your data is to figure out what is the measurement metric for each variable. For categorical and ordinal variables, we suggest producing frequency tables. For continuous variables, there is a wide range of descriptive statistics and graphs.

6.2 DESCRIBING CATEGORICAL AND ORDINAL VARIABLES

As we discussed in Chapter 6 of *FPSR*, a frequency table is often the best way to numerically examine and present the distribution of values for a categorical or ordinal variable. In Stata, the "tabulate" command is used to produce frequency tables. In a do-file or from the command line, the syntax for this command is:

```
tabulate variable
```

where "*variable*" is the name of the variable for which you want the frequencies.[1] This command produces a four-column table in which the first column contains the variable values (or value labels if there are value labels for this variable), the second column is the number of cases in the data set that take on each value, the third column is the percentage of cases that take on each value, and the fourth column is the cumulative percentage of cases from top to bottom. The data presented in Table 6.1 of *FPSR* are an example of the output obtained from using the "tabulate" command. These results were generated using the data set ANES2004small.dta which can be found in the

---

[1] When lines of computer code presented in this book contain a word or words in *italics*, those words are meant to be replaced by a specific word selected by the writer of the code. For instance, the word "*variable*" in the preceding line of code should be replaced with the name of specific variable in the data set that is loaded into Stata.

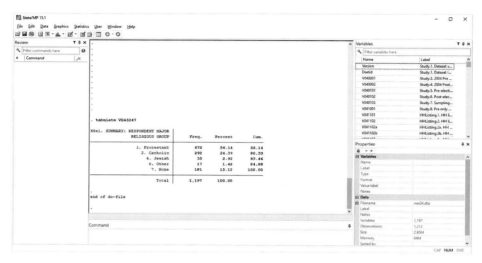

Figure 6.1: Raw output from "`tabulate`" command

Stata directory at www.cambridge.org/fpsr. The output from this use of the "`tabulate`" command is displayed in Figure 6.1. Take a moment to compare the table in Figure 6.1 with Table 6.1 of *FPSR*. Although both tables convey the same information, Table 6.1 of *FPSR* does so in a more polished fashion. This is an example of why we don't want to copy from the Stata output and paste that into our papers or presentations. Instead, it is important to craft tables so that they convey what is most necessary and don't include a lot of extra information. We'll have more to say about making tables in Chapter 8 (and forward) in this workbook.

Pie graphs, such as Figure 6.1 in *FPSR*, are a graphical way to get to know categorical and ordinal variables.[2] The syntax to produce a pie graph in a do-file or from the command line is:

```
graph pie, over(variable)
```

As an example of this, we can create a bar graph like that in Figure 6.2 of *FPSR* with the following line of code:

```
graph pie, over(V043247) scheme(s1mono)
```

which will produce a pie graph like the one displayed in Figure 6.2. Although this pie graph looks pretty good, we do not need the numbers displayed next to each category of the variable in the legend of Figure 6.2. One way around this is to add syntax to the command line that tells Stata what we want for each entry in the legend by rewriting the command as:

```
graph pie, over(V043247) /*
*/ legend(label (1 "Protestant") label (2 "Catholic") label (3 "Jewish") /*
```

---

[2] Once you've created a graph in Stata, which opens as a new window, you can click on that graph and use Stata's Graph Editor to customize the axis labels, colors, and the like. Try it!

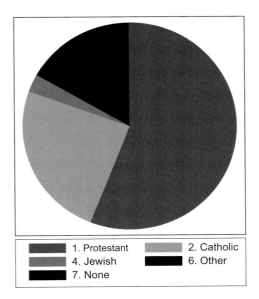

1. Protestant   2. Catholic
4. Jewish   6. Other
7. None

Figure 6.2: Initial pie graph

```
*/ label (4 "Other") label (5 "None")) /*
*/ scheme(s1mono)
```

where "legend" tells Stata that we want to change something in the legend under the pie and "label" tells Stata that what we want to change is the label. Note that the numbers displayed in Figure 6.2 are the values for the different categories of our religion variable while the numbers next to each "label" statement refer to the order of the legend entries from top left to bottom right.

As we discuss in Chapter 6 of *FPSR*, statisticians strongly prefer bar graphs to pie charts because bar graphs, especially when they have been sorted by the frequency with which the value occurs, make it easier for one to make assessments about the relative frequency of different values. The easiest way to obtain a figure like this in Stata is to run the following two commands:

```
generate variable1=variable2
graph bar (count) variable1, over(variable2, sort((count) variable1)
descending)
```

where "*variable1*" is the name of the variable for which you want the frequencies displayed in a bar graph, and "*variable2*" is the same variable duplicated. As an example of this, we can create a bar graph like that in Figure 6.2 of *FPSR* with the following lines of code:

```
gen V043247A=V043247
graph bar (count) V043247, /*
*/ over(V043247A, sort((count) V043247) descending) scheme(s1mono)
```

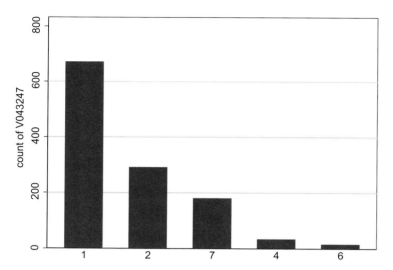

Figure 6.3: Initial bar graph

This would produce the bar graph displayed in Figure 6.3. Note, though, that Figure 6.3 is not exactly like Figure 6.2 of *FPSR*. To produce this figure, we need the following command:

```
graph bar (count) V043247, /*
*/ ytitle("Number of Cases") scheme(s1mono) /*
*/ over(V043247A, sort((count) V043247) descending /*
*/ relabel(1 "Protestant" 2 "Catholic" 3 "None" 4 "Jewish"
5 "Other"))
```

where, as we have seen before, "ytitle" tells Stata that we want to make our own label for the vertical axis, and "relabel" tells Stata that we want to provide text labels for each of the bars instead of the numbers that it places by default along the horizontal axis of the figure.

6.3   DESCRIBING CONTINUOUS VARIABLES

While the values for categorical variables in a sample of data can easily be presented in a frequency table, this is usually not the case for continuous variables. Consider Table 6.2 in *FPSR*. To produce this table, we ran the following two commands for the variable *incumbent vote* (which we named "inc_vote" in the data set):

```
sort inc_vote
list year inc_vote
```

where "sort" tells Stata to sort the observations in our data set from smallest value to the largest value of a particular variable and "list" tells Stata that we want to see, in the output window, the values of a particular variable or set of variables whose names we provide. Even for a relatively small data set, such as that presented in Table 6.2 in *FPSR*, this output provides a lot of information. For this reason, we turn to summary statistics when we want to describe continuous variables. To use a metaphor, with summary statistics, we are looking at the broad contours of the forest rather than examining each individual tree.

Figure 6.3 in *FPSR* displays the output from Stata's "summarize" command with the "detail" option. As we discuss in the book, this command produces a full battery of descriptive statistics for a continuous variable. The syntax for this command is:

```
summarize variable, detail
```

where the "detail" option tells Stata that we want a full set of output summarizing the values of a particular variable. From the discussion in Chapter 6, we can see that Stata's "summarize" command with the "detail" option presents both rank statistics and moment statistics to describe the values taken on by continuous variables. This command can also be used to produce summaries of the values for more than one variable by writing:

```
summarize variable1 variable2, detail
```

or, if we want this information for all variables in a data set, we would modify the command by simply leaving out the names of any variables and writing:

```
summarize , detail
```

though, if we want summaries of many or all of the variables in a data set, we recommend leaving off the "detail" option and writing simply:

```
summarize
```

An example of the output that this produces is displayed in Figure 6.4.

While statistical summaries of variables are helpful, it is also sometimes quite helpful to also look at visual summaries of the values for a variable. To get a visual depiction of rank statistics, we recommend producing a box–whisker plot like that displayed in Figure 6.4 in *FPSR*. The syntax for a box–whisker plot of the values for a single continuous variable is:

```
graph box variable
```

To get a visual depiction of moment statistics, we recommend producing either a histogram – as in Figures 6.5 and 6.6 from *FPSR* – or a kernel density plot – Figure 6.7 from *FPSR*. The syntax for a histogram of the values for a single continuous variable is:

```
histogram variable
```

From a do-file or from the command line, the syntax for a kernel density plot of the values for a single continuous variable is:

```
kdensity variable
```

When students are learning about histograms and kernel density plots, a frequent question that they have is, "Which is better?" We don't have a definitive answer to

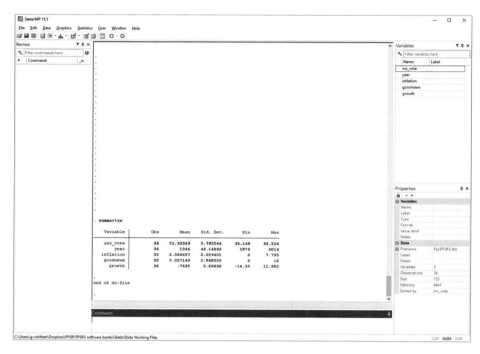

Figure 6.4: Output from the "`summarize`" command

this question. Both histograms and kernel densities are graphical ways for summarizing the distribution of values for one variable in a sample data set. As such, they both simplify reality. The histogram does this by dividing the different values for the variable being depicted into ranges called "bins" that look like the bars in a bar graph and then displaying the density of the number of cases within each of these ranges or bins. Kernel density plots, on the other hand, produce a more smoothed depiction of the contours of the forest of values for the variable being summarized. To go back to the metaphor that we started with, both histograms and kernel density plots are trying to summarize the broad shape of the forest and thus miss some of the details of individual trees. If you're having difficulty choosing which one you like better, one option is to put them both in the same figure. To do this, we can take advantage of the fact that both "`histogram`" and "`kdensity`" commands are specific members of Stata's comprehensive "`twoway`" graphics command. We can produce a single figure that combines a histogram and a kernel density plot for the same variable (in this case, *incumbent vote*) with:

```
twoway histogram inc_vote || kdensity inc_vote, scheme(s1mono)
```

in which "`twoway histogram`" tells Stata that we want to produce a graph from the "`twoway`" set of graphs and that the specific type of twoway graph that we want is a histogram, and the "`||`" is a way of telling Stata that we want the resulting figure to contain another twoway figure. Note that we do not need to repeat "`twoway`" in front of "`kdensity`" in this command. The resulting output is displayed in Figure 6.5. Although

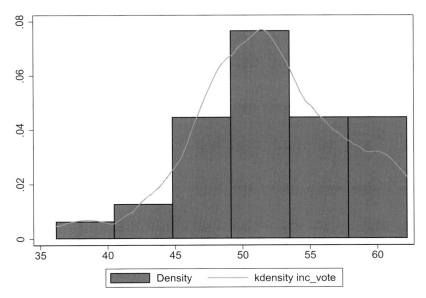

Figure 6.5: Initial figure combining a histogram and kernel density plot for incumbent vote

this figure looks pretty good, we don't particularly like the legend underneath. Since both a histogram and a kernel density plot are ways of showing the density of the values for a variable, we can get rid of this legend and label the vertical axis in this figure as density. This can be done with the following command:

```
twoway histogram inc_vote /*
*/ || kdensity inc_vote /*
*/ , scheme(s1mono) legend(off) ytitle("Density")
```

where "legend(off)" tells Stata that we do not want the legend and "ytitle("Density")" tells Stata how to label the vertical axis.

6.4   PUTTING STATISTICAL OUTPUT INTO TABLES, DOCUMENTS, AND PRESENTATIONS

So you've generated some statistical output for the first time. Congratulations! But now what do you do? As you can tell from the descriptions above, we think it's important to be thoughtful about how to present your results to your audience. That's why we went to great lengths to show you commands to make the graphics appear in the most interpretable way possible. The same is true with data that you wish to include in a tabular format. We emphasize that just copying and pasting output from Stata (or any other program) is unlikely to impress your audience – even if your audience is "just" your professor or teaching assistant.

For example, when we produce descriptive statistics in Stata using either the "tabulate" or "summarize" commands, we get a *lot* of output. Usually this output is much more than what we need to present in a paper that describes our variables one at a time. We therefore suggest making your own tables in whatever word processing program you are working with.

Graphs are a bit simpler, though. Once you have a graph that meets the standards we've outlined above, and you want to include it in a document, one of the easiest ways to do so is to right-click on the graph in Stata and select "copy" and then right-click on the location where you want to place the graph in your word processing program and select "paste." Depending on the word processor, you might just want to re-size the graphic image by clicking on the corner of the image and dragging the image to be bigger or smaller, depending on what would look best in your paper or presentation.

We'll have more to say about this topic in Chapter 8, and forward, as we introduce new statistical techniques to you. The upshot, though, is always the same: Put some care into what you present to your audience. The amount of attention you devote to the details – low or high – will be obvious to your audience.

6.5   EXERCISES

1. Open Stata and load the do-file named "Chapter 6 Categorical Variable Example.do" into the do-file editor. Make sure that you have the correct directory path for loading the data. In other words, if "C:\MyFPSRStataFiles" is not where you have your data, change this part of the do-file so that the data load into Stata.

    Once you have done this, run the code to produce the graphs presented in Figures 6.1 and 6.2 from *FPSR*. Open a word processing document and then copy these figures from Stata and paste them into your word processing document.

2. Run a "tabulate" command for variable V043093 which is each respondent's prediction of who will win the 2004 US Presidential Election. In your word processing document, create a frequency table like Table 6.1 from *FPSR* for variable V043093.

3. Create a pie chart and a bar graph like Figures 6.1 and 6.2 from *FPSR* for variable V043093. Copy these figures from Stata and paste them into your word processing document.

4. Write a short summary of what you see in the table and figures that you created using variable V043093.

5. Open Stata and load the do-file named "Chapter 6 Continuous Variable Example.do" into the do-file editor. Make sure that you have the correct directory path for loading the data. In other words, if "C:\MyFPSRStataFiles" is not where you have your data, change this part of the do-file so that the data load into Stata.

    Once you have done this, run the code to create a box–whisker plot, a histogram, kernel density plot, and a combined histogram and kernel density plot. Copy and paste each of these figures into your word processing document.

6.   Run a "summarize" command for the variable "growth" which is the percentage change in real (meaning that this measure is adjusted for inflation) gross domestic product (GDP) per capita (meaning that it has been adjusted for population). Make a table in your word processing document which contains the moment statistics for this variable.

7.   Produce a box–whisker plot for the variable "growth."

8.   Produce a histogram, kernel density plot, and a combined histogram and kernel density plot for the variable "growth." Copy and paste each of these figures into your word processing document.

9.   Write a short summary of what you see in the table and figures that you created using variable "growth."

7 PROBABILITY AND STATISTICAL INFERENCE

7.1 OVERVIEW

In this chapter, we teach you how to use two different computer simulations – one using a module in Stata, and another using a pre-programmed Excel spreadsheet. The goal of this chapter is to familiarize you with some of the basics of how probability works, and especially to see how sample sizes come into play.

7.2 DICE ROLLING IN STATA

Stata has a free add-on software package that users can install to simulate the rolling of dice. To find and install the package, launch Stata and type:

```
search dice
```

in the command window and hit enter. A help box will pop open as in Figure 7.1.

It's a rather long list of search results, and we have to scroll down a good bit before finding the correct embedded link to click. So scroll perhaps three-quarters of the way down in the search results box, and click on the blue text "dice from https://stats.idre.ucla.edu/stata/ado/tozip2014/teach/stata-teaching-tools-dice-rolling-simulation in Figure 7.2.

Finally, on the resulting menu, click on the blue text "[click here to install]" – as shown in Figure 7.3 – and the program will install. When it's done, close the installation box by clicking on the X in the top-right corner of the box.

You do need to have the administrative rights to install software on whatever computer you're working on. If this is your own personal computer, presumably this is not problematic. If you're on a lab computer at your college or university, you might need to have a lab worker assist you.

Once installed, running Stata's Dice package is easy. As always, if you need reminders about the commands, you can type:

```
help dice
```

in the command window and hit enter. The program contains three options:

1. The number of rolls of the dice (option "nr," with the default set to 10)
2. The number of dice rolled (option "nd," with the default set to 2)
3. The number of sides on each die (option "ns," with the default being 6)

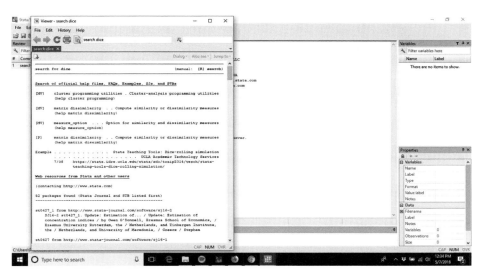

Figure 7.1: Search results for Stata's Dice program

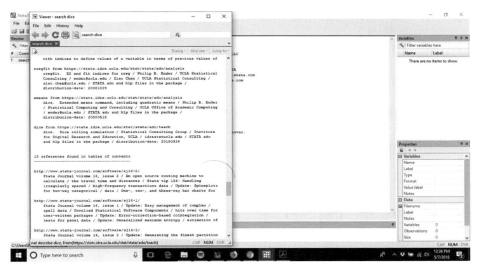

Figure 7.2: Scrolling down in the search results for Stata's Dice program

Every time you run the Dice program in Stata, it clears the data in memory (including any previous times you've rolled the dice). The program simulates the rolling of the dice the pre-specified number of times, and produces a bar chart with the output of the sum (if applicable) of the rolls.

For example, let's say we wanted to roll one six-sided die 300 times. We'd type the following in the command window of Stata:

```
dice, nr(300) nd(1)
```

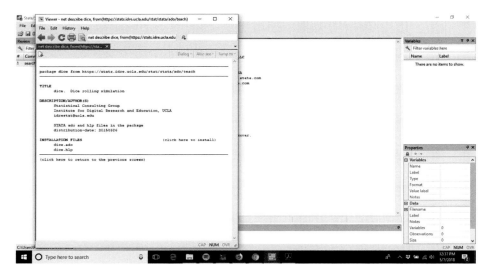

Figure 7.3: Installing Stata's Dice program

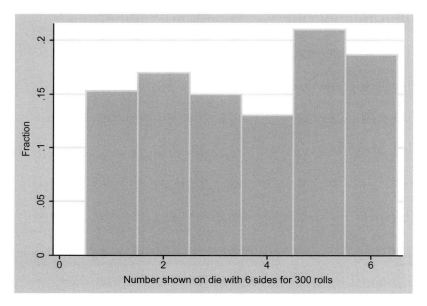

Figure 7.4: The results of 300 rolls of a six-sided die

and hit enter. (In this case, we can omit the "ns(6)" portion of the command because the default is a six-sided die.) The resulting bar chart with the rolls is shown in Figure 7.4.

The *x* axis in the figure represents the six sides of the die, and the *y* axis represents the proportion of the rolls that came out with that number. Of course, when you do this yourself on your own computer, you will get a different outcome, because the presented results are the result of random forces. In our roll, however, what you'll notice is that

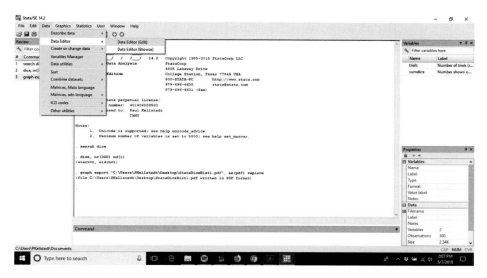

Figure 7.5: Accessing the results of our dice rolls in Stata

we rolled fewer 4s than we would have expected – about 0.13, or 13%, when we would have expected just under 17% of the rolls to come up 4. Among other things, the figure also reveals that, randomly, we rolled more 5s – about 0.21, or 21%, when we would have expected just under 17% – than would have been predicted by chance. Such is the nature of randomness.

Stata stores the rolls as a new data set. You'll notice that, after rolling the dice as we did, there are now two variables listed in the "Variables" window in the top right of your Stata program. Those variables are named *trials* and *sumdice*. The *trials* variable is just the roll number – from 1 to 300, in our case – and the *sumdice* variable is the sum of the dice – in our case, we only rolled one die, so there's no summation involved. We can open that data set the way we have learned before, under the "Data" menu, then "Data Editor," and "Data Editor (Browse)." See Figure 7.5.

Doing that, as you can see in Figure 7.6, opens up the data editor. You can see, there, that our first roll was a 3, the second was a 2, and so on.

We can, of course, learn more about our rolls of dice with the "summarize" command that we learned in Chapter 6. In the command window, typing:

```
summarize sumdice
```

and hitting enter will generate some simple statistics for our rolls of the dice. Those are presented in Figure 7.7.

The mean of our rolls – 3.633333, according to the output – is higher than would have been expected. (Right?) The standard deviation – which, as you will recall, measures how tightly clustered or how widely dispersed the scores are – is 1.744237.

Using the results of the central limit theorem from the textbook, we can use these figures to create a confidence interval for the likely value of the population mean based on what we have observed in our sample. To do that, we need to calculate the standard

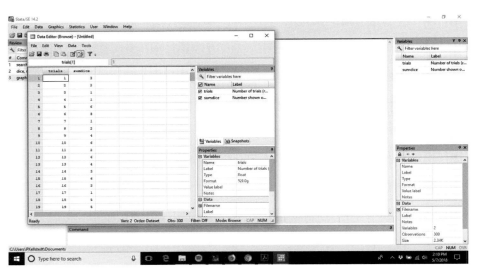

Figure 7.6: The data editor, with the results of our dice rolls in Stata

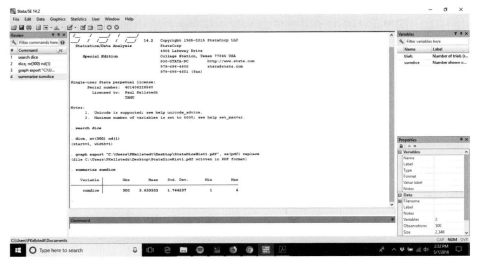

Figure 7.7: Summarizing the results of our dice rolls in Stata

error of the mean. You may recall that the formula for the standard error of the mean ($\sigma_{\bar{Y}}$) is

$$\sigma_{\bar{Y}} = \frac{s_Y}{\sqrt{n}},$$

where s_Y is the sample standard deviation and n is the sample size. In our case, that equals

$$\sigma_{\bar{Y}} = \frac{1.744237}{\sqrt{300}} = 0.10.$$

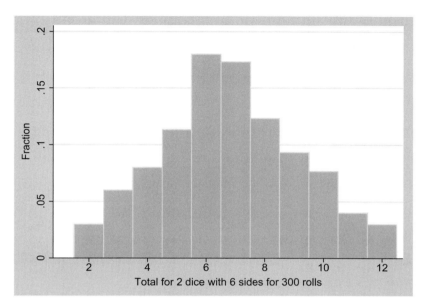

Figure 7.8: The results of 300 rolls of two six-sided dice

To create a 95% confidence interval for the likely value of the population mean, you will recall that we would use the rule of thumb that we would go two standard errors in both directions to obtain the interval. In other words,

$$\bar{Y} \pm 2 \times \sigma_{\bar{Y}} = 3.63 \pm (2 \times 0.10) = 3.63 \pm 0.20.$$

That means, based on what we've observed in our sample, we are 95% confident that the population mean for our rolls of the die lies somewhere on the interval between 3.43 and 3.83. There is a 2.5% chance that the true population mean is below 3.43, and a 2.5% chance that the true population mean is above 3.83.

Of course, you'll be able to tweak this exercise by varying the number of rolls of the die. When you do, it will change that number in the denominator. The larger the sample size, the larger the denominator in the formula, which means that the resulting quotient will be smaller. That smaller quotient translates to a tighter (smaller) confidence interval. This is how larger sample sizes reduce our uncertainty about the true value of the population characteristics in which we're interested.

Let's do one more example. Say that instead of rolling one die 300 times, we rolled two dice 300 times apiece. We would type the following in the command window of Stata:

```
dice, nr(300)
```

and hit enter. (This time, we can omit both the "ns(6)" portion of the command, as well as the "nd(2)" portion, because the default is to roll two dice.) The resulting bar chart with the rolls is in Figure 7.8.

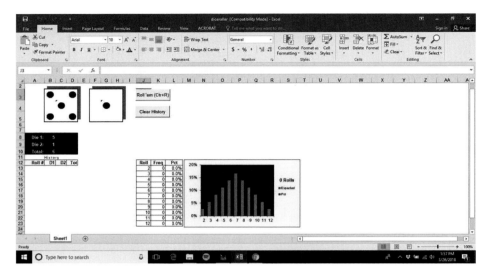

Figure 7.9: The dice roller in Excel

The x axis represents the sum of the rolls of the two dice, which means it ranges between 2 and 12. As before, the y axis displays the proportion of rolls in each category. The pattern, we're sure you'll notice, is quite different in Figure 7.8 than it was in Figure 7.4, in which we rolled only one die.

7.3   DICE ROLLING IN EXCEL

There is a variety of free spreadsheets available online that simulate the rolling of dice.[1] The one we will use is available at the following URL:

www.cambridge.org/FPSRstata

Right-click on the filename "diceroller.xls" where it says "DOWNLOAD" and save it to your computer.[2] Find the file and open it. What you'll see should look like Figure 7.9.

The spreadsheet is quite simple: It contains a basic program that simulates the rolling of two six-sided dice, with a graphic display of the resulting dice faces, as well as output data to keep track of the rolls. The sheet basically contains three sections. In the top-left of the sheet are the two dice. In the launch screen in Figure 7.9, those dice are a 5 and a 1. There are also buttons there to roll the dice – you can click the "Roll 'em (Ctrl+R)" button or press "Ctrl" and "R" on your keyboard. You can click the "Clear History" button to erase the history of rolls and start over.

The history of rolls of the two dice is displayed along the lower-left side of the sheet. In that section, there are columns of data to correspond to the roll number ("Roll #"),

---

[1] Google "spreadsheet dice roller" to find several of them.

[2] Unfortunately, the functionality of the spreadsheet only works in Microsoft Excel, so if you're used to using Google Sheets, you'll need to be on a computer that has Microsoft Excel installed on it.

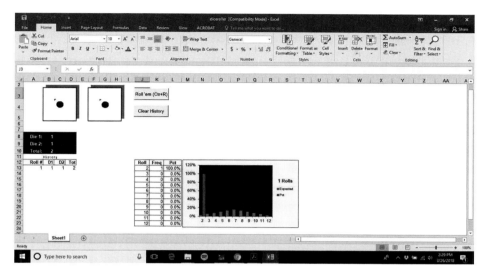

Figure 7.10: The results of our first roll

the roll of die 1 ("D1"), the roll of die 2 ("D2"), and the sum of die 1 and die 2 ("Tot"). In Figure 7.9, since we haven't rolled the dice yet, you will see that in the rows beneath the display of "Roll #, D1, D2, Tot," the cells are all empty. When we begin rolling the dice, those rows will begin to fill up.

The third section of the sheet, in the lower-right, shows the actual sum of the two dice (from the "Tot" column) – which will appear in red bars – as well as the distribution that we would *expect* to see given that the dice are fair – shown in gray bars.

Let's go ahead and roll the dice, either by hovering your mouse over the "Roll 'em" button and left-clicking it or hitting "Ctrl" and "R" on your keyboard. The results of our first roll are in Figure 7.10. As you can see, we rolled a "snake eyes" – a 1 and a 1. (Obviously, when you're doing this on your own computer, you might roll something different!) All of the output looks as you'd expect. In the lower-left of the sheet, you see that, for roll 1, die 1 was a "1" and die 2 was also a "1," making the total (the sum) "2" (because 1 plus 1 equals 2). That's reflected in the graph on the lower-right portion of the sheet, with a large red bar at the spot for "2," indicating that all 100% of rolls so far totaled a "2."

Let's click "Roll 'em" a few more times, so that we get ten rolls in total.

Figure 7.11 shows the results of the first ten rolls that we performed when writing this chapter. (Again, the outcomes of your rolls are quite likely to be different than ours!) You'll notice from the figure that we haven't rolled another "snake eyes." In fact, we've rolled three "4"s, two "6"s, and the other five results just one apiece.

We can roll the dice as many times as we'd like. (Just press "Ctrl" and "R" on your keyboard repeatedly. Yes, that means pressing it 100 times if you want 100 rolls, or 1000 times if you want 1000 rolls.) Go ahead and roll the dice around 100 times, and watch the red and gray bars shift as you do. (For our purposes right now, it doesn't matter if you roll them exactly 100 times.)

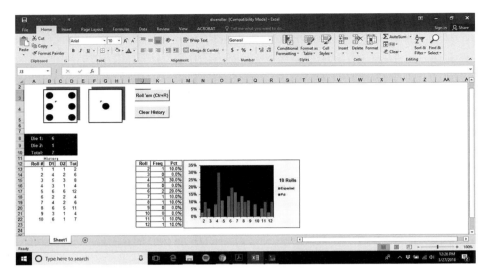

Figure 7.11: The results of our first ten rolls

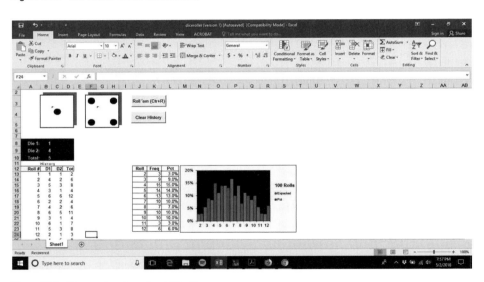

Figure 7.12: The results of our first 100 rolls

Figure 7.12 shows our results. As always, your rolls will be different from the ones we got. Let's examine the results in the figure. As you can see from the output screen and associated bar graph, we have rolled a total of 4 – either through a 1 and a 3, or a pair of 2s, or a 3 and a 1 – 15 times out of 100. That's more than would be expected by chance. You can also see that we've managed to roll double-6s six times out of the 100 rolls – again, more than would be expected. Perhaps the biggest discrepancy between the observed outcomes in red and the expected ones in gray is in the rolls that total 8. For whatever reason, we rolled about half as many 8s as would have been expected by chance.

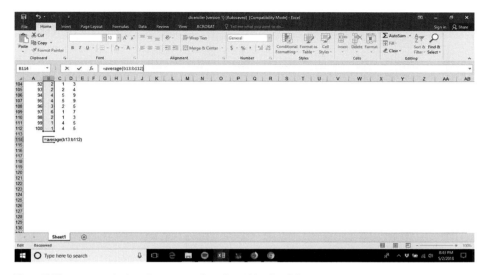

Figure 7.13: How to calculate the average of our first 100 rolls of die 1

Let's be clear: None of the above is meant to imply a judgment – positive or negative – on what we've found. In theory, there are a "squadpillion" possible rolls of these two dice, and what we've just done is sample one, then ten, and then 100 of them. At the extreme, rolling the two dice just one time produced a rather odd – by definition! – "outcome." Every single roll (of that one roll!) was a 2! How weird is that? Of course, for a single roll, *any* outcome would have been "odd" in this sense. As we move from one roll to ten to 100, though, we start to see the beginning of convergence between what we observe and what we expect to observe. Will the observed outcomes ever *exactly* equal the expected ones? Probably not.

One other thing that Excel allows us to do is to calculate the averages of the rolls of the individual die, and of the dice collectively. Doing so is straightforward. For example, if we want to calculate the average of the rolls of die 1, we can go anywhere in the spreadsheet and type:

```
=average(b13:b112)
```

and hit the "enter" key on the keyboard. (You'll see that we performed this in cell b114, because it is below the bottom of the string of cells for which we are calculating the mean, with a single space in between the last cell of data – cell b112 – and where we want our mean to be displayed.) That process is displayed in Figure 7.13, before we hit the "enter" key. When we hit the "enter" key, of course, the result will appear.

As you can see in Figure 7.14, the average of our 100 rolls of die 1 is 3.47. (We repeat the admonition that, when you perform this in your own spreadsheet, you will almost certainly get different results.) When we repeat the process – that is, type:

```
=average(c13:c112)
```

in cell c114 – for die 2, we find a different result, as is evident in Figure 7.15.

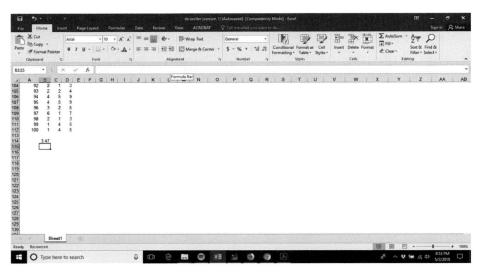

Figure 7.14: The result of calculating the average of our first 100 rolls of die 1

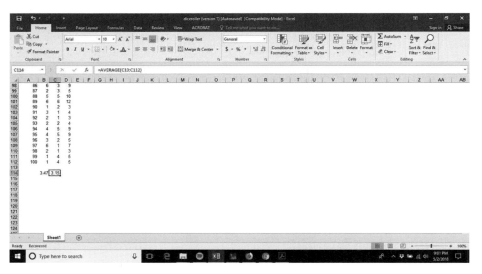

Figure 7.15: The result of calculating the average of our first 100 rolls of die 2

That mean is 3.15. Does that figure seem "too low" to you? (And why did we type "too low" in scare quotes just there?) Obviously, in a mathematical sense, the result of 3.15 for die 2 is lower than the outcome of 3.47 for die 1: $3.15 < 3.47$, we all know. We have computed the average of the sum of die 1 and die 2 in column D.

That result is displayed in Figure 7.16, and shows that the mean is 6.62. Because the mean of the rolls of die 1 is 3.47, and the mean of the rolls of die 2 is 3.15, the fact that the mean of the sum is 3.62 should not be surprising ($3.47 + 3.15 = 3.62$).

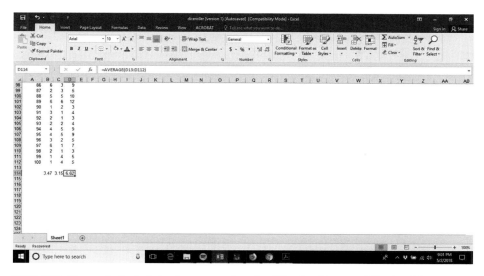

Figure 7.16: The result of calculating the average of our first 100 rolls of the sum of dice 1 and 2

7.4   EXERCISES

1.   In the Stata dice roller, roll a single six-sided die 500 times. Produce a histogram of the output, and calculate the mean and standard deviation of the sample. On the basis of those results, calculate (by hand) the 95% confidence interval for the population mean.

2.   In the Stata dice roller, show the effects of the sample size on the size of the confidence interval for the population mean by rolling two six-sided dice the following number of times:

   (a)   9 times
   (b)   25 times
   (c)   100 times
   (d)   400 times
   (e)   1600 times
   (f)   2500 times

   Describe in some detail the nature of the effects of sample size on the amount of uncertainty we have connecting a sample to the underlying population. **Bonus:** Use Stata to input data into two variables. Let the first variable be the sample sizes above, and the second variable be the resulting standard error of the mean. Plot the relationship graphically. (Hint: You might need to peek ahead to Chapter 8 to see how to do this!)

3.   For the above question, how (if at all) does changing the sample size affect the calculated sample means and standard deviations? Can you explain why?

4.   In Figure 7.9 from the dice rolling module in Excel, before we actually roll any dice, what should we *expect* the mean of a set of rolls of a single die to be? Why? And what should we expect the mean of the sum of two rolls of

dice to be? Why? How do these numbers compare to the outcomes we found in Figures 7.14, 7.15, and 7.16?

5.   In Figure 7.10, you notice that we happened to roll two 1s. Given that, what is the probability of rolling two 1s on the next roll? Explain your answer.

6.   You've surely noticed that the gray bars in the dice rolling module in Excel – representing the "expected" rolls – in all of the dice figures seem to be shaped almost like a normal distribution. Why is that? Be careful in answering this question, and try to be as explicit as possible in arriving at your answer.

7.   If you haven't already, in the dice rolling module in Excel, roll your die 100 times. What are the means of die 1, die 2, and the sum of the two? How do these numbers compare to the outcomes we found in Figures 7.14, 7.15, and 7.16? What do you make of these similarities or differences?

8.   Using the dice rolling module in Excel, roll the dice until the "observed" bars (in red) *roughly* approximate the gray "expected" bars. How many rolls did it take? Print out (or take a screen shot of) your output and turn it in with your answer.

8 BIVARIATE HYPOTHESIS TESTING

8.1 OVERVIEW

We are now ready to start testing hypotheses! As we discuss in Chapter 8 of *FPSR*, bivariate hypothesis tests, or hypothesis tests carried out with only two variables, are seldom used as the primary means of hypothesis testing in political science research today. But it is imperative to understand the basic mechanics of bivariate hypothesis tests before moving to more complicated tests. This same logic applies to the use of statistical computing software. In this chapter, we teach you how to conduct hypothesis tests using the three techniques presented in Chapter 8 of *FPSR*: tabular analysis, difference of means, and the correlation coefficient.

8.2 TABULAR ANALYSIS

In tabular analysis, we are testing the null hypothesis that the column variable and row variable are unrelated to each other. We will review the basics of producing a table in which the rows and columns are defined by the values of two different variables, generating hypothesis-testing statistics, and then presenting what you have found.

The Stata syntax for producing a two-variable table is:

```
tab2 rowvariable colvariable, column
```

where "*rowvariable*" is usually the dependent variable (with its values displayed across rows in the table) and "*colvariable*" is usually the independent variable (with its values displayed down the columns in the table). The option "column" tells Stata that, in addition to the frequency of values (or number of cases) being displayed in each cell, this command should produce column percentages for each row beneath the frequencies. As detailed in Chapter 8 of *FPSR*, these column percentages allow for the comparison of interest – they tell us how the dependent variable values differ in terms of their distribution across values of the independent variable. It is crucial, when working with tables of this nature, to put the appropriate variables across the rows and columns of the table and then to present the column frequencies. For example, to recreate Table 8.2 in *FPSR* we first run the command:

```
tab2 V2Trump unionHH, col
```

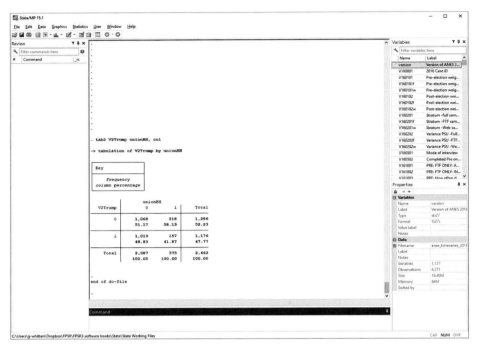

Figure 8.1: Raw output from "`tab2`" command

where "V2Trump" is a categorical variable that takes on a value of "1" if the respondent reported voting for Donald Trump and "0" if the respondent reported voting for Hillary Clinton, and "unionHH" is a variable that takes on a value of "1" if the respondent reported that someone in their household belonged to a union and "0" otherwise. The output from this running command is displayed in Figure 8.1. Take a moment to compare this raw output with Table 8.2 in *FPSR*. There are three notable differences. First, in order to isolate the numbers needed for the assessment at hand (whether or not voters from union households voted differently from voters from nonunion households in the 2016 election), we need only the column percentages. Second, instead of the names of the variables from the output ("V2Trump" and "unionHH") and the numbers reflecting their values ("1" and "0"), we have provided more intuitive labels for the variables and their values. And, third, we have added a note making it clear what are the values reported in each cell of the table.

8.2.1   Generating Test Statistics

In Chapter 8 of *FPSR* we discuss in detail the logic of Pearson's chi-squared test statistic which we use to test the null hypothesis that the row and column variables are not related. To get this test statistic and the associated *p*-value for a two-variable table in Stata from a do-file or from the command line, the syntax for producing a two-variable table is:

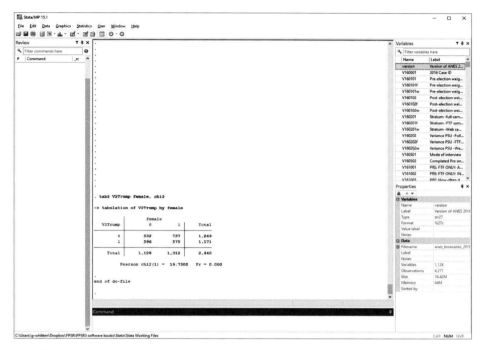

Figure 8.2: Raw output from "tab2" command

```
tab2 rowvariable colvariable, chi2
```

where, again, "*rowvariable*" is usually the dependent variable (with its values displayed across rows in the table) and "*colvariable*" is usually the independent variable (with its values displayed down the columns in the table). The option "chi2" tells Stata to report a chi-squared test statistic and the associated *p*-value. Thus to conduct the chi-squared test reported in Section 8.4.1 of *FPSR*, we would issue the command:

```
tab2 V2Trump female, chi2
```

which produces the output displayed in Figure 8.2.

8.2.2 Putting Tabular Results into Papers

We recommend that you make your own tables in whatever word processing program you choose to use instead of copying and pasting the tables that you make in Stata. The first reason for doing so is that you will think about your results more closely when you are producing your own tables. This will help you to catch any mistakes that you might have made and to write more effectively about what you have found. Another reason for doing so is that tables constructed by you will tend to look better. By controlling how the tables are constructed, you will be able to communicate with maximum clarity.

As a part of making your own tables, you should have the goal in mind that your table communicates something on its own. In other words, if someone *only* looked at your table, would they be able to figure out what was going on? If the answer is "yes," then you have constructed an effective table. We offer the following advice ideas for making useful tables:

- Give your tables a title that conveys the essential result in your table
- Make your column and row headings as clear as possible
- Put notes at the bottom of your tables to explain the table's contents

8.3   DIFFERENCE OF MEANS

Difference of means tests are conducted when we have a continuous dependent variable and a limited independent variable.

8.3.1   Examining Differences Graphically

When we use graphs to assess a difference of means, we are graphing the distribution of the continuous dependent variable for two or more values of the limited independent variable. Figure 8.1 of *FPSR* shows how this is done with a box–whisker plot. The syntax for doing this is:

```
graph box depvariable, over(indvariable)
```

where "*depvariable*" is the name of the continuous dependent variable and "*indvariable*" is the name of the limited independent variable. The code for producing Figure 8.1 of *FPSR* is:

```
graph box govttime, /*
*/ over(mingov, relabel(1 "majority" 2 "minority")) /*
*/ ytitle("Number of Days in Government") scheme(s1mono)
```

where the variable "govttime" is the number of days each government lasted in office and "mingov" is a categorical variable equal to 1 if the government was a minority government and equal to 0 otherwise.[1]

In Figure 8.2 of *FPSR* we produced a kernel density plot of the distribution of our continuous dependent variable for the two values of our limited independent variable. The syntax for producing this figure involves Stata creating two separate plots and overlaying them. The syntax for doing this is:

```
twoway kdensity depvariable if indvariable condition /*
*/ ‖ kdensity depvariable if indvariable condition
```

where, as before, "*depvariable*" is the name of the continuous dependent variable and "*indvariable*" is the name of the limited independent variable. The "*condition*" in this case is that the independent variable is equal to a particular value. The "‖" in the command above tells Stata that you are going to overlay a second twoway plot. The code for producing Figure 8.2 of *FPSR* is:

---

[1] The "/*" and "*/" in the above commands indicate a multi-line command.

```
twoway kdensity govttime if mingov==1 || kdensity govttime if
mingov==0, /*
*/ legend(label(1 "minority") label(2 "majority")) /*
*/ xtitle("Number of Days in Government") scheme(s1mono)
```

where "if mingov==1" and "if mingov==0" are the two "*condition*" statements which tell Stata to plot only the kernel density for cases for which each condition is met. Stata reads the "==" as "is exactly equal to."

8.3.2   Generating Test Statistics

To conduct a difference of means t-test such as the one discussed in Chapter 8 of *FPSR*, the syntax is:

```
ttest depvariable, by(indvariable)
```

For the t-test that we present in Chapter 8 of *FPSR*, the syntax is:

```
ttest govttime, by(mingov)
```

which produces the output displayed in Figure 8.3. In Figure 8.3, we can see that the output from a difference of means t-test like this produces a lot of output. The first part of this output is a table of descriptive statistics for the dependent variable across each value of the independent variable and then overall. Much of this information is presented in Table 8.11 of *FPSR*. We then get the t-statistic for the test (3.44) that we presented in *FPSR* and the p-value for the associated hypothesis test.[2]

8.4   CORRELATION COEFFICIENTS

Correlation coefficients summarize the relationship between two continuous variables. They are also an important building block to understanding the basic mechanics of two-variable regression models.

8.4.1   Producing Scatter Plots

We can examine the relationship between two continuous variables in a scatter plot such as Figure 8.3 in *FPSR*. The syntax for producing such a figure is:
```
twoway scatter depvariable indvariable
```
If we run this code for our running example of economic voting with incumbent vote as the dependent variable and economic growth as the independent variable:
```
twoway scatter inc_vote growth, scheme(s1mono)
```

---

[2] You will notice that there are three hypothesis tests presented at the bottom of Figure 8.3. The one that we present in *FPSR* is the middle one which is expressed as "`Ha: diff != 0`" and for which Stata reports a p-value of 0.0007. In Chapter 10 of *FPSR* we get deeper into the business of different types of hypotheses and, more specifically, the difference between a hypothesis test like the one that we conducted and hypothesis tests like the others listed in Figure 8.3.

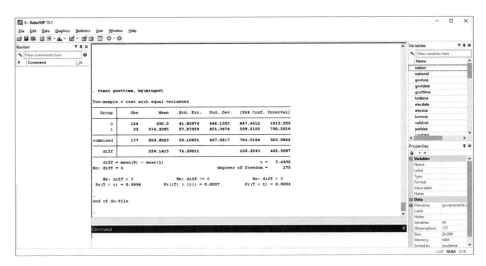

Figure 8.3: Raw output from "ttest" command

we get the graph displayed in Figure 8.4. The code for producing Figure 8.3 in *FPSR* is:

```
twoway scatter inc_vote growth, /*
*/ ytitle("Incumbent Party Vote Percentage" " ") /*
*/ xtitle(" " "Percentage Change in Real GDP Per Capita") /*
*/ msymbol(Oh)/*
*/ scheme(s1mono)
```

where the double quotes with a space between them are an easy way to get a little space between axis labels and the figure to which they apply, and "msymbol(Oh)" tells Stata to make large hollow circles instead of the default filled circles that we see in Figure 8.4. These symbols make it a little bit easier to see overlapping data points.

8.4.2   Generating Covariance Tables and Test Statistics

To generate the output for a covariance table like Table 8.13 in *FPSR*, the syntax is:

```
correlate variable1 variable2, covariance
```

As you can probably guess, "correlate" is a command that can be used to produce correlation coefficients and the option "covariance" produces a covariance table. Continuing with the same running example, we can produce the output needed to create Table 8.13 in *FPSR* by running:

```
correlate inc_vote growth, covariance
```

The raw output from running the following command:

```
pwcorr depvariable indvariable, cov
```

generates the output that we see in Figure 8.5. As you might imagine, we can also use the "correlate" command to generate a table of correlation coefficients between any two

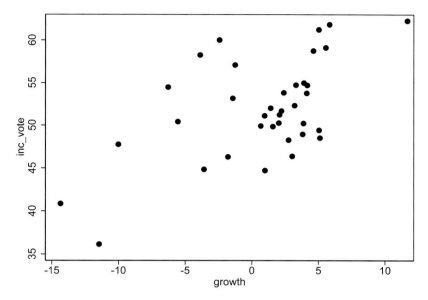

Figure 8.4: Basic output from "`scatter`" command

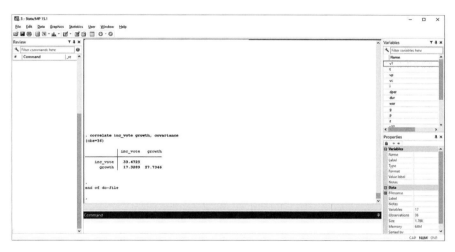

Figure 8.5: Basic output from "`correlate`" command with the "`covariance`" option

or more continuous variables.[3] To generate a correlation coefficient with the associated
p-value, the syntax is:

```
pwcorr variable1 variable2, sig
```

---

[3] The "pw" in `pwcorr` stands for "pairwise." When examining the relationship between two variables, the
"`correlate`" and "`pwcorr`" commands will yield identical results. However, if multiple variables are
investigated, the coefficients can be different for reasons having to do with missing data. Also, the two
commands have somewhat different options. Type "`help pwcorr`" for more information.

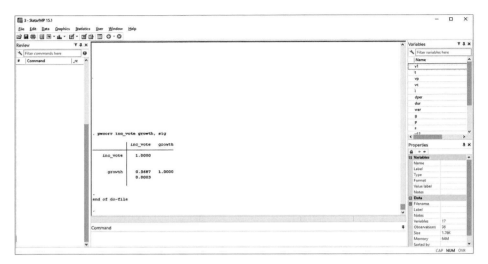

Figure 8.6: Basic output from "`pwcorr`" command with the "`sig`" option

where the command "`pwcorr`" is short for "pairwise correlations" and can be used to obtain the correlation coefficients for more than two pairs of variables. The "`sig`" option tells Stata that we want the p-value reported underneath each correlation coefficient. So, if we submit the command:

```
pwcorr inc_vote growth, sig
```

we will get the output that is displayed in Figure 8.6, which includes the correlation coefficient (0.5687) that we calculate in Chapter 8 of *FPSR* together with its associated p-value (0.0003).

8.5   EXERCISES

1. Open Stata and load the do-file named "Chapter 8 Tabular Analysis Example.do" into the do-file editor. Make sure that you have the correct directory path for loading the data. In other words, if "C:\MyFPSRStataFiles" is not where you have your data, change this part of the do-file so that the data load into Stata.

    Once you have done this, run the code to produce the example output presented in Section 8.2 of this book.

    (a)   Calculate a chi-squared test for the output presented in Figure 8.1. Report the results of this test and write about what it tells you about the theory that voters in union households are more likely to support candidates from the left.

    (b)   A commonly expressed theory of politics is that people who are dissatisfied with the performance of the legislature are more likely to vote for candidates who are political outsiders. Test this theory with a hypothesis test using the variables "StronglyDisapproveCongress" (coded as "1" if the respondent reported that they strongly disapprove of the way that Congress was doing its job) and "V2Trump." Produce an appropriate table to show what you have found and report the results from a chi-squared test for the hypothesis test. Write about what this analysis tells you about the theory in question.

2. Open Stata and load the do-file named "Chapter 8 Difference of Means Example.do" into the do-file editor. Make sure that you have the correct directory path for loading the data. In other words, if "C:\MyFPSRStataFiles" is not where you have your data, change this part of the do-file so that the data load into Stata.

    (a) Once you have done this, run the code to produce Figures 8.1 and 8.2 from *FPSR*. Copy and paste these figures into your word processing document.

    (b) A commonly expressed theory of politics is that governments which contain the party which got the most votes at the last election have more of an electoral mandate and thus will last longer. Test this theory with a hypothesis test using the variables "eptyplur" (coded as "1" if the party which received the most votes was in the government and "0" otherwise) and "govttime." Produce appropriate figures and a table to show what you have found and report the results from a *t*-test for the hypothesis test. Write about what this analysis tells you about the theory in question.

3. Open Stata and load the do-file named "Chapter 8 Covariance and Correlation Example.do" into the do-file editor. Make sure that you have the correct directory path for loading the data. In other words, if "C:\MyFPSRStataFiles" is not where you have your data, change this part of the do-file so that the data load into Stata.

    (a) Once you have done this, run the code to produce Figure 8.3 from *FPSR*. Copy and paste this figure into your word processing document.

    (b) As we discuss in *FPSR*, there are many different ways to measure economic performance, the independent variable in the theory of economic voting. Go through the steps that we go through in the lab but replace the variable "growth" with "inflation." Produce an appropriate figure and a table to show what you have found and report the results from a *t*-test for the hypothesis test on the correlation coefficient. Write about what this analysis tells you about the theory of economic voting.

9 TWO-VARIABLE REGRESSION MODELS

9.1 OVERVIEW

In Chapter 9 of *FPSR* we introduce the two-variable regression model. As we discuss, this is another two-variable hypothesis test that amounts to fitting a line through a scatter plot of observations on a dependent variable and an independent variable. In this chapter, we walk you through how to estimate such a bivariate model in Stata.

9.2 ESTIMATING A TWO-VARIABLE REGRESSION

The estimation of a two-variable regression model, as discussed in Chapter 9 of *FPSR*, is fairly straightforward. The syntax is:

```
regress depvariable indvariable
```

where "regress" is the command which tells Stata to estimate a regression model, "*depvariable*" is the name of the dependent variable, and "*indvariable*" is the name of the independent variable. This will produce output such as that pictured in Figure 9.5 of *FPSR*. In that example, the command, which appears in the top of the figure, was:

```
reg inc_vote g
```

where "reg" is a shortened version of the "regress" command which told Stata to estimate a two-variable regression with "*inc_vote*," the variable name for the measure of incumbent vote, as the dependent variable, and "*g*," the variable name for economic growth, as the independent variable. Note that for the exercises in this workbook, we have renamed our independent variable from "g" in the example pictured in Figure 9.5 of *FPSR* to "growth."

9.3 GRAPHING A TWO-VARIABLE REGRESSION

To better understand what is going on in a two-variable regression model, it is often helpful to graph the regression line. An example of this is presented in Figure 9.4 of *FPSR*. The code for producing that figure is:

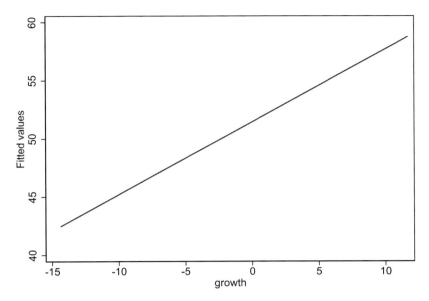

Figure 9.1: Basic output from the "`twoway lfit`" command

```
twoway (scatter inc_vote growth) /*
*/ (lfit inc_vote growth, lcolor(black)), /*
*/ ytitle("Incumbent Party Vote Percentage") /*
*/ xtitle("Percentage Change in Real GDP Per Capita") /*
*/ legend(off) /*
*/ xline(.7635, lcolor(black) lpattern(dash) lwidth(thin)) /*
*/ yline(51.92569, lcolor(black) lpattern(dash) lwidth(thin)) /*
*/ scheme(s1mono)
```

There is obviously a lot going on in this command. As we have moved deeper into this book, we have produced increasingly complicated figures. Rather than writing the many lines of code for a figure such as Figure 9.4 of *FPSR* all at once, most researchers will start off with a simple figure, and then gradually add additional details.

We will now walk through an example of how to do this using Figure 9.4 of *FPSR*. First, we want to have the linear fit of the model as a line in our figure. This can be done in Stata by issuing the following command:

```
twoway lfit depvariable indvariable
```

where "`twoway lfit`" tells Stata that we want to produce a twoway graph which shows the linear fit of a two-variable regression model. Issuing the following command:

```
twoway lfit inc_vote growth, scheme(s1mono)
```

produces output like what we see in Figure 9.1. Next, we want to add a scatter plot which shows the location of each of our observations around the regression line. To do this, we now need to tell Stata that we want to have two different types of twoway graphs

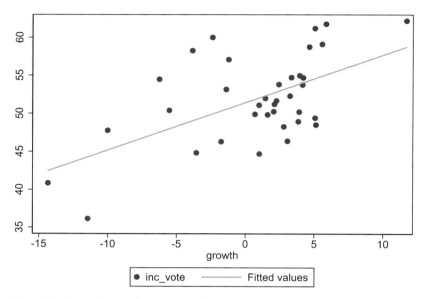

Figure 9.2: Output from the "`twoway lfit`" command together with "`twoway scatter`"

together in the same figure. This can be done by first writing the command "`twoway`," and then writing the two or more separate twoway commands each within parentheses without the word "`twoway`" in front of them. So, keeping with our running example, the command:

```
twoway (scatter inc_vote growth) (scatter inc_vote growth),
scheme(s1mono)
```

would tell Stata to produce output like what we see in Figure 9.2. This output certainly shows us the main components of the regression model, with incumbent vote as the dependent variable and growth as the independent variable. For Figure 9.4 of *FPSR*, we wanted to show that the estimated regression line for a two-variable regression always passes through the intersection of the means of the dependent variable and the independent variable. To get these means, we used the "`summarize`" command which we introduced in Chapter 6 of this book. We can then add a vertical line showing the mean of growth with an "`xline`" option and a horizontal line showing the mean of vote with a "`yline`" option. In both cases, the location on the axis at which we want the line to appear has to be written in parentheses immediately after the option. So, to keep building to our running example, the syntax:

```
twoway (scatter inc_vote growth) (scatter inc_vote growth), /*
*/ xline(.7635) yline(51.92569) /*
*/ scheme(s1mono)
```

would tell Stata to produce output like what we see in Figure 9.3.

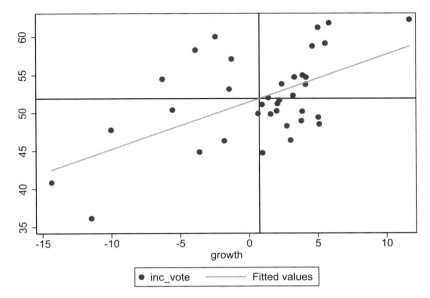

Figure 9.3: Output from the "twoway lfit" command together with "twoway scatter" and "mean" lines

If we return to the command which produced Figure 9.4 of *FPSR*:

```
twoway (scatter inc_vote growth) /*
*/ (lfit inc_vote growth, lcolor(black)), /*
*/ ytitle("Incumbent Party Vote Percentage") /*
*/ xtitle("Percentage Change in Real GDP Per Capita") /*
*/ legend(off) /*
*/ xline(.7635, lcolor(black) lpattern(dash) lwidth(thin)) /*
*/ yline(51.92569, lcolor(black) lpattern(dash) lwidth(thin)) /*
*/ scheme(s1mono)
```

the remaining parts of the command that we have not discussed in earlier chapters are the following fairly straightforward refinements:

- "lcolor(black)" inside "(lfit inc_vote growth, lcolor(black))" tells Stata that we want the regression line to be drawn in black rather than the gray which we see in Figures 9.1 through 9.3,
- "legend(off)" tells Stata that we do not want the legend box which appears under Figures 9.2 and 9.3,
- the "lpattern" options tell Stata the pattern that we want for a particular line, and
- the "lwidth" options tell Stata the width that we want for a particular line.

9.4   EXERCISES

1.   Open Stata and load the do-file named "Chapter 9 Two-Variable Regression Examples.do" into the do-file editor. Make sure that you have the correct directory path for loading the data. In other words, if "C:\MyFPSRStataFiles" is not where you have your data, change this part of the do-file so that the data load into Stata. Once you have done this, run the code to produce Figure 9.4 from *FPSR*. Copy and paste this figure into your word processing document.

2.   If we change the independent variable from our running example from growth to inflation, what would the theory of economic voting lead us to expect in terms of a hypothesis for the slope of a regression line with variable inc_vote as the dependent variable and inflation as the independent variable? Explain your answer.

3.   Estimate a regression model with the variable inc_vote as the dependent variable and inflation as the independent variable.

    (a)   Copy and paste this output into your word processing document.

    (b)   Write about the results from the hypothesis test that you discussed above. What does this tell you about the theory of economic voting?

    (c)   Produce a figure like Figure 9.4 from *FPSR* but with inflation as the independent variable (inc_vote should remain as the dependent variable). Copy and paste this figure into your word processing document.

10 MULTIPLE REGRESSION: THE BASICS

10.1 OVERVIEW

In Chapter 10 of *FPSR*, we introduce the multiple regression model in which we are able to estimate the effect of X on Y holding Z constant. Here, we show you how to execute such models in Stata.

10.2 ESTIMATING A MULTIPLE REGRESSION

The estimation of a multiple regression model, as discussed in Chapters 10 and 11 of *FPSR*, is just an extension of the command used for estimating a two-variable regression. For example, if we have three independent variables, the syntax is:

```
regress depvariable indvariable1 indvariable2 indvariable3
```

where "*depvariable*" is the name of the dependent variable, and the terms that begin with "*indvariable*" are the names of the independent variables.[1] For Stata's multiple regression command, the name of the dependent variable must always come first, followed by the names of the independent variables. The order in which the independent variables appear does not matter; you will get the same results regardless of their order.

The command to estimate the multiple regression displayed under the column titled "C" in Table 10.1 of *FPSR* is:

```
regress inc_vote growth goodnews
```

which produces output like that displayed in Figure 10.1.

10.3 FROM REGRESSION OUTPUT TO TABLE – MAKING ONLY ONE TYPE OF COMPARISON

As we discuss in Section 10.9 of *FPSR*, when presenting the results from more than two regression models in the same table, it is important that we set up our

---

[1] In this example of the syntax, we have chosen to show the syntax for having three independent variables. In practice, you may have as many independent variables as you want in a regression model as long as you meet the minimum mathematical requirements that each independent variable varies, $n > k$, and you have no perfect multicollinearity. The first two of these requirements are discussed in Section 9.5 and the third is discussed in Section 10.7 of *FPSR*.

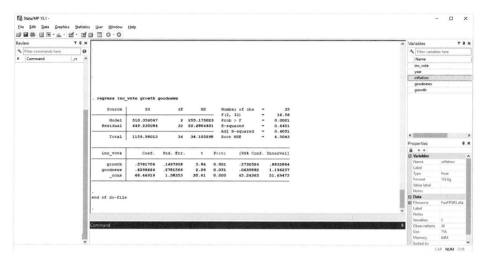

Figure 10.1: Basic output from a multiple regression

comparisons appropriately – either as comparisons of different model specifications estimated with the same sample of data, or the same model specification estimated with different samples of data. This is because if both the sample of data and the model specification change, then we cannot know for sure whether any differences in the estimates that we are observing are due to the different sample or the different specification.

10.3.1   Comparing Models with the Same Sample of Data, but Different Specifications

If your data set doesn't have any missing values for any of the variables that you want to include in a set of models with different specifications, then making a table for such comparisons is pretty straightforward. All that you need to do is to estimate the regressions of interest to you and put them into separate columns of a table. If, as is often the case, you have some missing values for some of the variables that you are including in your different models, then you need to take some extra steps in order to make sure that the regressions that you are comparing are all estimated with the exact same observations.

As an example of this, we will use the regressions that were used to produce the results presented in Table 10.1 of *FPSR*. If you compare the output presented in Figure 10.1 with that presented in Figure 9.5 of *FPSR*, one thing that you might notice is that the regression presented in Figure 9.5 of *FPSR* has 36 observations, whereas the regression presented in Figure 10.1 has 35. This is the case because the variable goodnews is missing for the 1876 election. Thus to obtain the output presented in Table 10.1 of *FPSR*, it is necessary to exclude the observation for 1876 from the model that we estimate to produce the results presented in column "**A**" of Table 10.1 of *FPSR*. One way to do this, given that we know the year of the observation that we want to exclude, would be to write the command as:

```
regress inc_vote growth if year != 1876
```

which tells Stata to estimate a regression with "inc_vote" as the dependent variable and "growth" as the independent variable using *only* those observations for which the condition after the "if" statement is met. In this case, the condition is "year != 1876" which translates into "year is not equal to 1876."

But what would we do if we didn't know exactly which observations are missing particular values of particular independent variables?[2] One of the easiest ways is just to estimate the model using all cases that are not missing for any of the independent variables that you plan to include in the models that you want to present. In our running example, we would estimate the following two models:

```
regress inc_vote growth if goodnews != .
regress inc_vote goodnews if growth != .
```

where " != ." in each command translates into "is not equal to missing." These two commands, together with the following command:

```
regress inc_vote growth goodnews
```

create the output presented in Table 10.1 of *FPSR*.

10.3.2   Comparing Models with the Same Specification, but Different Samples of Data

As an example of how to compare models with the same specification, but different samples of data, let's imagine that we want to look at our the results from our running example of economic voting in the United States for the observations after World War II compared with all observations before then. Although there are some different interpretations of when the war started, most people agree that World War II ended in 1945. So, to estimate models on samples of data after the war and all other cases, we would estimate the following two models:

```
regress inc_vote growth goodnews if year > 1945
regress inc_vote growth goodnews if year < 1945
```

where the commands are identical except for the conditions written after the "if."

10.4   STANDARDIZED COEFFICIENTS

In order to obtain standardized coefficients, as discussed in Section 10.5 of *FPSR*, you can add a comma and the word "beta" to the multiple regression syntax:

```
regress depvariable indvariable1 indvariable2indvariable3, beta
```

---

[2] If an observation is missing for the dependent variable, it will not be included in any of the models that we estimate. Also, in general, we should have gotten to know our data before we estimate a regression model, and part of getting to know one's data is figuring out what are the missing values and why they are missing.

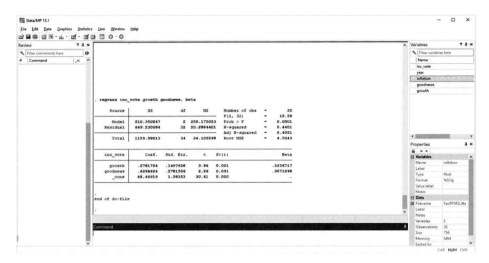

Figure 10.2: Basic output from a multiple regression with the "beta" option

To estimate such a model with "inc_vote" as our dependent variable, and "growth" and "goodnews" as our independent variables, using:

```
regress inc_vote growth goodnews, beta
```

we will get output like that displayed in Figure 10.2.

10.5   EXERCISES

1. Open Stata and load the do-file named "Chapter 10 Multiple Regression Examples.do" into the do-file editor. Make sure that you have the correct directory path for loading the data. In other words, if "C:\MyFPSRStataFiles" is not where you have your data, change this part of the do-file so that the data load into Stata. Once you have done this, run the code to produce the output shown in Figure 10.1. Copy and paste this figure into your word processing document.

2. Estimate a multiple regression model with both inflation and growth as the independent variables and inc_vote as the dependent variable. Estimate the two two-variable models needed to make a table like Table 10.1 of *FPSR* where you are comparing the results across three specifications on the same sample of observations. Put your results into a table in your word processing document and write about what you have found.

3. Estimate the two multiple regression models described in this chapter with the same specification but where the sample is divided according to whether the observation occurred before or after 1945. Put these results into a table in your word processing document and write about what you have found.

4. Estimate a multiple regression model with standardized coefficients with good news, inflation, and growth as the independent variables and inc_vote as the dependent variable. Put your results into a table in your word processing document and write about what you have found.

11 MULTIPLE REGRESSION MODEL SPECIFICATION

11.1 OVERVIEW

In Chapter 11 of *FPSR* we discuss a series of issues that researchers commonly encounter when they are trying to test their theories using multiple regression models. The advice for how to proceed when one encounters these issues involves a series of additional commands in Stata, which we detail in this chapter.

11.2 DUMMY VARIABLES

As we discuss in Section 11.2 of *FPSR*, dummy variables are variables that take on one of two different values. The vast majority of the time in political science, these two values are "zero" and "one." Dummy variables are usually created and named so that "one" represents the presence of a condition and "zero" represents the absence of that condition. In order not to confuse the people who will be reading your work or watching your presentations, it is a good idea to follow these conventions. For example, if you have a dummy variable to identify the gender identity of a survey respondent, it might be tempting to call the variable "gender." That, however, would leave unclear the issue of what the zeros and ones represent. If, by contrast, you named your variable "female," then the convention would be that a zero is for male respondents – or the absence of the condition "female" – and one is for the female respondents – the presence of the condition "female."

11.2.1 Creating a Dummy Variable with the "generate" and "replace" Commands

Sometimes data sets that you are working with come with proper dummy variables already created for you. When they do not, you will need to create your own variables. There are multiple ways to create dummy variables in Stata. In general, we recommend that you first create a new variable with all of its values set to missing. In Stata, the "generate" command tells Stata that you want to create a new variable and the code for a missing value is a period ".", so the command:

```
generate newvariable=.
```

will create a new variable with all missing values. We can then use the "replace" command to replace the missing values with the appropriate values that we want. For instance, if the dummy variable that we want to create is from an existing variable with values of 7 and 9 which we want to make 1 and 0, respectively, we would use the following syntax:

```
replace newvariable=1 if oldvariable==7
replace newvariable=0 if oldvariable==9
```

which tells Stata to replace the missing values in "*newvariable*" with 1 if the "*oldvariable*" was equal to 7 and to replace the missing values in "*newvariable*" with 0 if the "*oldvariable*" was equal to 9. Stata reads the "==" in the two commands above as "is exactly equal to."[1]

Whenever you create a new variable, it is critically important to check that you created exactly what you intended to create. One way to check this is with a "tab2" command, which we introduced in Section 8.1.1. In this case, we could check our work with the command:

```
tab2 oldvariable newvariable
```

which tells Stata to create a two-variable table with the non-missing values of "*newvariable*" and "*oldvariable*."

So, to create the data for the example in Section 11.2 of *FPSR*, we first load the Stata data set named "ANES1996small.dta," which is a subset of the 1996 American National Election Study. From the codebook for this study, we can tell that coding of values for each respondent's self-identified gender is in the variable named "V90066" and that the values of this variable are equal to 1 for "male" and 2 for "female." To check the values for this variable, we submit the command:

```
tab V90066, missing
```

Having seen that there are only values equal to 1 and 2, we can now create the variable "female" and check what we have created using the following commands:

```
generate female=.
replace female=0 if v960066==1
replace female=1 if v960066==2
tab2 v960066 female, missing
```

The output from these commands is displayed in Figure 11.1.

---

[1] As is often the case, there are many different ways to create new variables in Stata. One more succinct way to adjust the values of a new variable that you create is to use the "recode" command. This command allows you to change all of the values of a new variable in a single line of code. While this is a quicker way to get things done, we have found that new users often make more mistakes when using the "recode" than they do when they use the "replace" command and make one change per line of code.

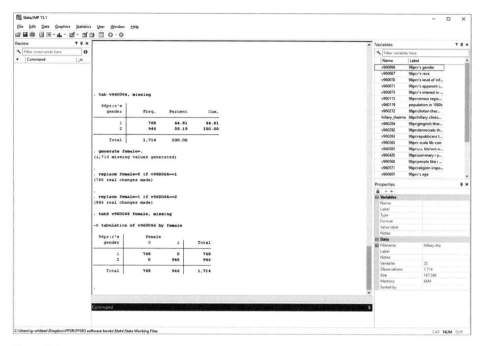

Figure 11.1: Output from creating a dummy variable

11.2.2   Estimating a Multiple Regression Model with a Single Dummy Independent Variable

As we discussed in Section 10.2 of this software book, the syntax for estimating a multiple regression with three independent variables is:

```
regress depvariable indvariable1 indvariable2 indvariable3
```

where "*depvariable*" is the name of the dependent variable, and "*indvariable*" terms are the names of the three independent variables. When we have only a single dummy independent variable, then we just simply add the name of that variable to the list after "*depvariable*."

As an example of this, we can estimate the regression model displayed on the left side of Table 11.1 of *FPSR* with the following command:

```
regress hillary_thermo income female
```

where "hillary_thermo" is the dependent variable, respondents' thermometer ratings of Hillary Clinton, "income" is a continuous independent variable, and "female" is the dummy independent variable that we just created. Note that, as was the case with our multiple regression models with multiple continuous independent variables, the order of the independent variables does not matter for this command. The output from this command is displayed in Figure 11.2.

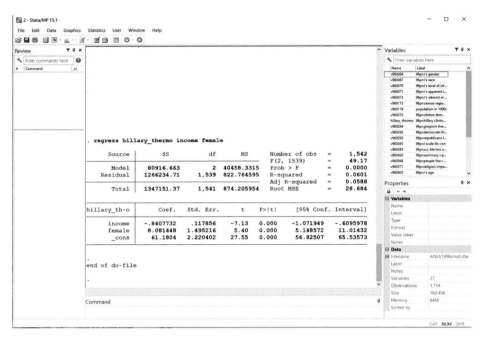

Figure 11.2: Output from a regression model with a dummy variable

11.2.3   Estimating a Multiple Regression Model with Multiple Dummy Independent Variables

To estimate a multiple regression model with multiple dummy variables, you use the same command syntax as in the previous section. The main complication comes when the multiple dummy variables represent values for a categorical variable with more than two values. As we discuss in Section 11.2.2 of *FPSR*, in such a case, in order to avoid what is known as the "dummy variable trap," you need to leave one category of such an independent variable out of the regression model, and that omitted category becomes the "reference category."

11.3   DUMMY VARIABLES IN INTERACTIONS

In Section 11.3 of *FPSR*, we discuss testing interactive hypotheses with dummy variables. There are several different ways to do this in Stata. We recommend that you use a fairly straightforward approach where you start out by creating a new variable that is the multiplicative interaction between the dummy variable and the continuous variable. The syntax for creating a new variable that is the product of two variables already in the data set is:

generate *newvariable=oldvariable1*oldvariable2*

where "*newvariable*" is the name of the interaction, "*oldvariable1*" and "*oldvariable2*" are the names of the dummy variable and the continuous variable that you wish to interact (the order of them does not matter), and "*" tells Stata to multiply the values of these two variables.

To estimate a multiple regression with this interaction, you would use the following syntax:

regress *depvariable newvariable oldvariable1 oldvariable2*

which could also include more independent variables in addition to "*oldvariable1*" and "*oldvariable2*." As with all multiple regressions, the order of the independent variables in such a command line does not matter.

So, to create the interactive model displayed on the right side of Table 11.6 of *FPSR*, we first create the interaction between the continuous variable "womenmvmt_thermo," thermometer scores for the women's movement, and the dummy variable "female" with the following code:

generate womenmvmt_thermo_female = womenmvmt_thermo*female

We can then run the following command to produce the desired regression output:

regress hillary_thermo womenmvmt_thermo female womenmvmt_thermo_female

The output from this command is displayed in Figure 11.3.

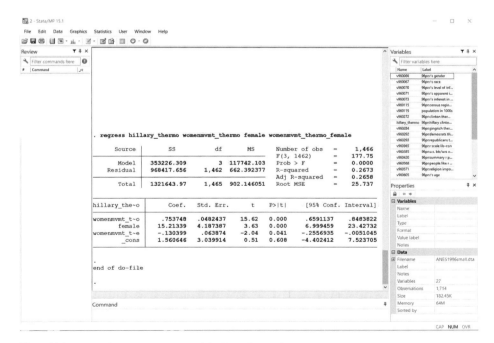

Figure 11.3: Output from a regression model with an interaction

11.4   POST-ESTIMATION DIAGNOSTICS IN STATA FOR OLS

In Chapter 11 of *FPSR* we discuss a number of diagnostic procedures that can be carried out once an ordinary least-squares (OLS) model has been estimated. These procedures are all available in Stata. It is important to keep in mind that, when asked to conduct such an analysis, Stata will always do so using information from the most recent regression model that was estimated.

11.4.1   Identifying Outliers and Influential Cases in OLS

Figure 11.4 in *FPSR* shows the results from an "lvr2plot" which is short for "leverage-versus-residual-squared plot." The syntax for producing this type of figure on the last estimated regression model is:

lvr2plot

It is often the case that we want to identify which cases are at the extremes in our "lvr2plot". This can be done by using a variable that identifies the individual cases. The syntax for doing this is:

lvr2plot, mlabel(*idvariable*)

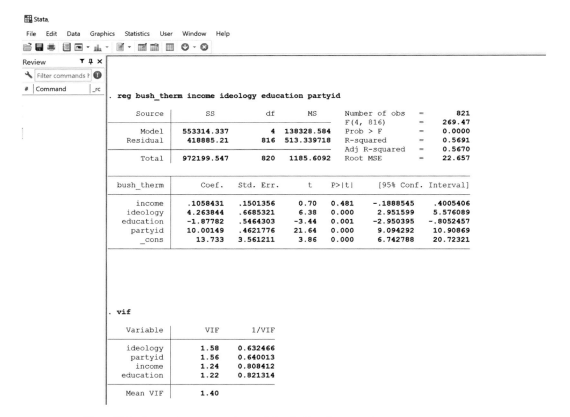

Figure 11.4: Output from a regression model and a "vif" command

where ", mlabel" tells Stata that we want to use the "mlabel" option, which is a graphics option to display the values of a variable for each case next to that case, and "*idvariable*" is the name of the variable whose values we wish to display.

Table 11.8 in *FPSR* shows the five largest DFBETA scores from a regression model. The syntax for estimating DFBETA scores is:

```
predict newvariable, dfbeta(indvariable)
```

where "*newvariable*" is the name of a new variable that will be created containing the DFBETA value for each observation, and "*indvariable*" is the name of the independent variable for which you want to have the DFBETA calculations made.

To create the example outputs in Figure 11.4 in *FPSR*, we start out by running the following command:

```
regress BUCHANAN GORE
```

which creates the regression displayed in Table 11.7 of *FPSR*. Having done this, the information from this regression model is now sitting in Stata's memory. We can then use this information to produce an "lvr2plot" by running the following command:

```
lvr2plot
```

and we can run the following command:

```
lvr2plot, mlabel(COUNTY)
```

to produce the "lvr2plot" that is displayed in Figure 11.4 of *FPSR*. We can produce Figure 11.5 of *FPSR* by first running the following line of code:

```
predict yhat, xb
```

which tells Stata to create a new variable named "yhat" and the option "xb" tells Stata that we want that new variable to equal the predicted values, the $\hat{Y}_i$ values, for each observation based on the results from the last regression model that we estimated.[2] We can then submit the following lines of code to produce Figure 11.5 of FPSR:

```
twoway (scatter BUCHANAN GORE, mlabel(COUNTY)) (line yhat GORE) /*
*/ , ytitle("Buchanan Vote") xtitle("Gore Vote") legend(off)
```

To produce the DFBETA scores that are presented in Table 11.8 of *FPSR*, we first submit the following command:

```
predict dfgore, dfbeta(GORE)
```

which tells Stata to create a new variable named "dfgore", and the option "dfbeta(GORE)" tells Stata that the new variable should be the DFBETA score for each observation for the independent variable "GORE." We can then sort the values of the new variable with this command:

```
sort dfgore
```

---

[2] The name "*xb*" for this option is shorthand for the operation that we are asking Stata to perform for us – multiplying the independent variable values for each observation, the "x," by the parameter estimates, the "b."

and get Stata to list all of the values from the largest negative value to the largest positive value with the following command:

```
list COUNTY dfgore
```

which lists the name of each county with the DFBETA scores that we calculated. Note that in Table 11.8 of *FPSR*, we listed only the five largest absolute value DFBETA scores.

Detecting Multicollinearity in OLS

As we discussed in Section 11.5 of *FPSR*, one way to detect multicollinearity is to estimate a variance inflation factor (or "VIF") for each independent variable after you have estimated your regression model. The syntax for producing this type of figure on the last estimated regression model is:

```
vif
```

To see an example of how we do this, we can estimate the regression that produces "Model 3" in Table 11.2 of *FPSR* with the following command:

```
reg bush_therm income ideology education partyid
```

If we then run a "vif" command, we will get the output which is displayed in Figure 11.4.

11.5   EXERCISES

1.   Open Stata and load the do-file named "Chapter 11 Multiple Regression Dummy Variable Examples.do" into the do-file editor. Make sure that you have the correct directory path for loading the data. In other words, if "C:\MyFPSRStataFiles" is not where you have your data, change this part of the do-file so that the data load into Stata. Once you have done this, run the code to produce the output shown in Figure 11.2. Copy and paste this into your word processing document.

2.   Run the code to produce the output shown in Figure 11.3. Copy and paste this into your word processing document.

3.   Create a dummy variable identifying male respondents. Estimate the model displayed in Figure 11.2 with this new variable instead of the variable identifying female respondents. Copy and paste this into your word processing document. Write a brief summary of what these results tell you.

4.   Create an interaction between the new dummy variables that you created to identify male respondents and the women's movement thermometer. Estimate the model displayed in Figure 11.3 with this new variable instead of the variables identifying female respondents. Copy and paste this into your word processing document. Write a brief summary of what these results tell you.

5.   Open the do-file named "Chapter 11 Outliers and Influential Cases Examples.do" Once you have done this and made sure that you have the correct data set loaded

into Stata, run the regression with votes for Buchanan as the dependent variable and votes for Gore as the independent variable. Copy and paste this output into your word processing document.

6. Run the code to produce the lvr2plot that is displayed in Figure 11.4 of *FPSR*. Copy and paste this figure into your word processing document.

7. Run the code to produce Figure 11.5 of *FPSR*. Copy and paste this figure into your word processing document.

8. Run the code to produce the DFBETA scores that are presented in Table 11.8 of *FPSR*. In your word processing document, list the DFBETA values for the five counties with the smallest (in absolute values) scores for this calculation together with their DFBETA scores.

9. Open the do-file named "Chapter 11 vif example.do." Once you have done this and made sure that you have the correct data set loaded into Stata, run the regression model and the vif command. Copy and paste this output into your word processing document.

12 LIMITED DEPENDENT VARIABLES AND TIME-SERIES DATA

12.1 OVERVIEW

In Chapter 12 of *FPSR* we discuss two important extensions to multiple regression models: models with dichotomous dependent variables and models with time-series data. In this chapter we provide an explanation of the commands needed to deal with these circumstances in Stata.

12.2 MODELS WITH DUMMY DEPENDENT VARIABLES

As we discuss in Chapter 12 of *FPSR*, there are several different models that can be used when we have a dummy dependent variable. In this set of examples, we will work with data from the 2004 American National Election Study (ANES) with a dependent variable named "Bush," which equals one for respondents who reported that they voted for George W. Bush and equals zero for those respondents who reported that they voted for John Kerry.[1] To get a look at the values for this variable, we can run a "tab" command:

```
tab Bush
```

As we discuss in Chapter 12 of *FPSR*, one option when we have a limited dependent variable is simply to run a regression model using the standard syntax that we discussed in Chapter 10 of this book. For example, if we have three independent variables, the syntax is:

```
regress depvariable indvariable1 indvariable2 indvariable3
```

and the only difference is that the "*depvariable*" is a dummy variable. So, if we want to estimate the model displayed in Table 12.1 of *FPSR*, we would write the command as:

```
regress bush partyid eval_WoT eval_HoE
```

where "bush" is the dependent variable for which the values are displayed in Figure 12.1, "partyid" is "Party Identification," "eval_WoT" is "Evaluation: War on Terror,"

---

[1] This is the same example that we use in Chapter 12 of *FPSR*. For a more detailed explanation of the variable and how it was created, see footnote 1 on page 274 of *FPSR*.

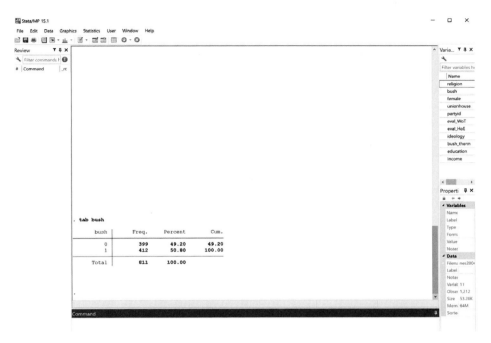

Figure 12.1: Table of values for the variable "Bush"

and "eval_HoE" is "Evaluation: Health of the Economy." To calculate and summarize the predicted probabilities from this model, we use the following commands with what should now be familiar syntax:

```
predict yhat, xb
summarize yhat, detail
```

which produces the output displayed in Figure 12.2. Looking at this output, we can see that when we create the new variable named "yhat," Stata gives us a message about missing values being generated. This is the case because Stata will only calculate the predicted values for those cases that were included in the regression model that we just estimated. If we look at the results from the "summarize" command, we can see that we get some predicted values (what we refer to as $\hat{P}_i$ values) that are greater than one. As we discuss in Chapter 12 of *FPSR*, one of the problems of the linear probability model is that it can produce predicted probabilities that are greater than one or less than zero. This is one of the main reasons why political scientists prefer to use either a binomial logit model or a binomial probit model when they have a dummy dependent variable.

To estimate a binomial logit model in Stata, the syntax is:

```
logit depvariable indvariable1 indvariable2 indvariable3
```

and to estimate a binomial probit model in Stata, the syntax is:

```
probit depvariable indvariable1 indvariable2 indvariable3
```

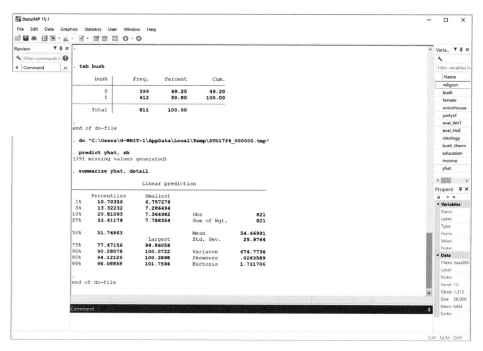

Figure 12.2: Calculating and displaying the predicted values from the linear probability model

As we discuss in Chapter 12 of *FPSR*, with each of these types of models there is an estimated systematic component for each observation, what we call the $X_i\hat{\beta}$ values, that can be put through a link function to produce predicted probabilities, what we refer to as $\hat{P}_i$ values. The command for calculating the $\hat{P}_i$ values after either a binomial logit or binomial probit has been estimated is:

```
predict newvariable, pr
```

where "*newvariable*" is the name of the new variable that we want to create, and the "pr" option tells Stata that we want the new variable to be the predicted probabilities for each of our observations that was included in the regression estimation.

So, to continue with our running example, we can produce the logit and probit columns of the results displayed in Table 12.2 of *FPSR* and predicted probabilities for each observation by running the following lines of code:

```
logit bush partyid eval_WoT eval_HoE predict p_BNL, pr
probit bush partyid eval_WoT eval_HoE predict p_BNP, pr
```

We can then display summary statistics for the resulting predicted probabilities by running the following lines of code:

```
summarize p_BNL, det
summarize p_BNP, det
```

which produces the output presented in Figure 12.3.

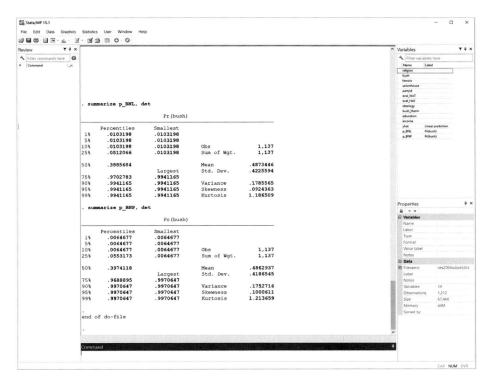

Figure 12.3: Summary statistics for predicted values from a binomial logit model and a binomial probit model

In order to produce classification tables like Table 12.3 in *FPSR*, we first need to create a new variable which is the predicted value of the dependent variable, what we have labeled "Model-based expectations" in Table 12.3. For the linear probability model in this example, we would use the following three separate lines of code:

```
gen p_vote_LPM=yhat
recode p_vote_LPM -.1/.5=0 .5000001/1.2=1
tab2 bush p_vote_LPM, cell
```

where we first create a new variable "p_vote_LPM" equal to the predicted values from the linear probability model that we estimated. We then recode the values of "p_vote_LPM" so that predicted probabilities of 0.5 or smaller become predictions that the individual will vote for Kerry (coded as zero) and predicted probabilities greater than 0.5 become predictions that the individual will vote for Bush (coded as one). We then produce a table of the values of actual vote and our model-based predictions. The output from these commands is presented in Figure 12.4.

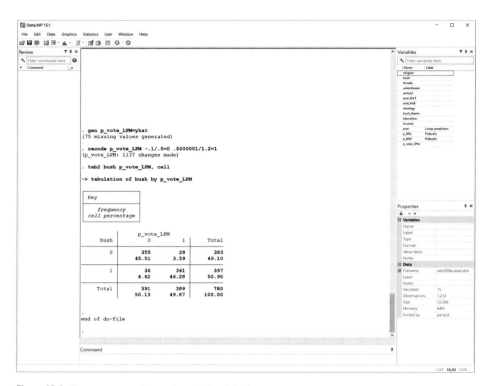

Figure 12.4: Raw output used to produce Table 12.3 of *FPSR*

12.3   BEING CAREFUL WITH TIME-SERIES DATA

The section title here might seem a bit ominous. Why, after all, do we suggest that you need to "be careful" with time-series data? What could possibly go wrong? From a scientific perspective, lots could go wrong. In this section, we'll raise some crucial issues and show you how to draw the most appropriate conclusions from the time-series data you have.

All of the issues revolve around the critical issue of *dependence*, by which we simply mean that the value of a variable at any time t "depends" to some varying (but important) degree on its own past values: at time $t - 1$, or perhaps even further back in its history. In Section 12.3.2 of *FPSR*, we described this as the *memory* of a series. The underlying principle at play in time-series analysis is that the more a variable's current value at time t depends on its past values at $t - 1$ (and further back), the more important it is to take the memory into account. Failing to do so makes it very likely – sometimes almost a certainty – to falsely find evidence of a causal relationship when one is not present in reality. (For example, consider the example in Section 12.3.3 of *FPSR* involving golf course proliferation and the demise of the nuclear family in the post-war United States.) In a nutshell, that's why you should "be careful" with time series.

12.3.1   Setting Up a Time-Series Data Set in Stata

This issue of dependence has lots of implications for how we should evaluate causal relationships involving time-series data. But it begins even before that. It has important (but simple) implications for how we set up a data set. To see why, consider a data set of cross-sectional data, where the cases are individual people responding to a survey. Typically, the individuals responding to a cross-sectional survey are selected randomly, which means that the presence of one individual from the underlying population does not affect the probability of another individual from the population being selected. That is, the selection of two different individual people from the population is *independent*. Picking one person doesn't affect the presence or absence of another person in the sample. As a result, when we consider the cases in our data set – the rows in the data file – the ordering of those rows doesn't matter. It makes no difference whether row 11 in our data file represents Friedrich from Frankfurt and row 12 represents Martina from Munich, or vice versa. Because the cases are presumed to be independent of one another, the ordering makes no difference whatsoever, and would have no effect on any statistical analyses we performed. That's not true in a time-series data set.

To see why, download the data set "Ch12TS.dta" from the *FPSR* web site, and open it. Follow along on your own computer as we execute the following commands.

Because the observations contain the aforementioned dependence, the ordering of them in our data set matters. And Stata will need to be told that the data set under consideration is a data set of ordered, time-series data. Figure 12.5 shows this for a data set of US President Bill Clinton's approval ratings over the 96 months of his two terms.

You'll notice in the data editor that the first row of the data represents observations for the value of *Year* as 1993 and *Month* as 1. So that monthly observation is for January

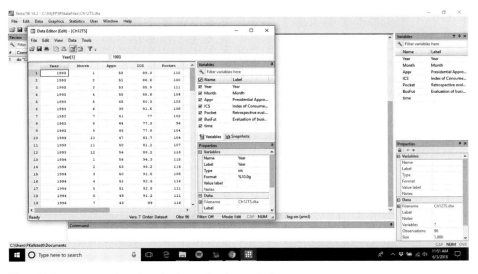

Figure 12.5: The data editor view of a time-series data set in Stata

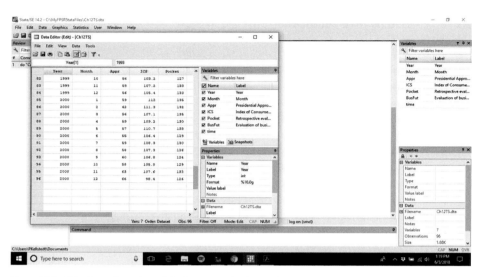

Figure 12.6: The data editor view of the last rows of a time-series data set in Stata

of 1993, which is when President Clinton was inaugurated. Because the ordering of observations is important, yes, it matters that the first observation (row 1) in the data set is the first observation in the time series. Equally important is that the second row, as you can see from Figure 12.5, represents February of 1993. And so on. The 96th and final row of the data set, shown in Figure 12.6, is for December of 2000, President Clinton's last full month in office.[2] In short, the ordering of the observations in a time-series data set matters.

Next, we need to tell Stata that these data are a time-series data set. (Yes, we have to tell Stata this. How else would it know?) Preliminarily, although we have a variable that represents *Year* and one that represents *Month*, we do not yet have one that represents year-and-month – like "January 1993." As it stands, we need two variables to convey this information. So we need to create a variable for time, which in this case will have the format *Year-and-Month*. We do that with the following command:

```
generate time=ym(Year,Month)
```

where "Year" and "Month" in the command are because the relevant columns in the data set from Figure 12.5 are called "Year" and "Month" (and, yes, these are case-sensitive). When we execute this command, we will have a new variable called "time" appear in our list of variables.

---

[2] The careful reader may have noticed that we used the word "full" in that sentence. President Clinton, of course, served until January 20, 2001. Thus it requires some care for the analyst to decide how to code polling observations from January 1–19, 2001. The same applies for the beginning of Clinton's first term, when George H.W. Bush was President for most of January 1993. In this case, we used only surveys in January 1993 after Clinton was inaugurated, and dropped any surveys in January 2001 before George W. Bush became president. The key point is not that you must do it this way, but that you must be careful and clear about such decisions.

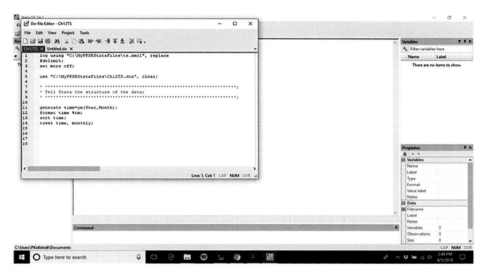

Figure 12.7: The beginning of a time-series .do file in Stata

Second, we need to tell Stata the format of those observations. We do that with the command:

```
format time %tm
```

The "%tm" at the end of the line tells Stata that the variable is a time variable, formatted monthly.[3]

Third, we need to insure that the data set is sorted by time, which we do by using the command:

```
sort time
```

Our last and most crucial command puts it all together, with:

```
tsset time, monthly
```

Obviously, the ", monthly" portion of the line is important here, and the "time" portion is because we named the variable "time" in our first command. (Again, "help tsset" at the command prompt gets you there.)[4]

We strongly recommend using do-files with such operations, where the above sequence of four commands come in a batch, just after opening the data file and declaring an output file. Such a do-file is pictured in Figure 12.7, and that do-file is included in the book's online resources along with the data sets.

---

[3] Stata's help system with the format command is very useful. Just type "help format" at the command prompt.

[4] If you're using the pull-down menus instead of a do-file or the command prompt, this last step can be found under the "Statistics" menu, then "Time Series," then "Setup and utilities," then "Declare dataset to be time-series data."

Figure 12.8: Output from executing "tsset" in Stata

Executing that batch of commands should produce output as in Figure 12.8. You'll notice, near the bottom of the output, the following reply from Stata:

```
time variable:  time, 1993m1 to 2000m12
       delta:  1 month
```

This serves as a check that everything has been executed properly. If we get anything back from Stata that does not correspond perfectly with the data that we've given it, then something is amiss.

12.3.2   Lag and Difference Operators in Stata

In Sections 12.3.1 through 12.3.4 of the main text, we introduced a couple of time-series concepts that are very important for estimating models – in particular, the notion of *lagged* values of a variable and that of the *first difference* of a variable.

Lagged values, you will recall from the text, are just represented with a change in the subscripts of a variable. For a variable that we denote Y_t, the value of that variable when it is lagged by one period is written Y_{t-1}. In Stata, if we have a variable "*Appr*" – in this data set, that variable represents a monthly reading of Bill Clinton's approval rating – then a one-period lag for that variable is simply:

```
l.Appr
```

And a variable representing a two-period lag is simply:

```
l2.Appr
```

And so on. (To be clear, the text before the period in the above two commands is a lower-case "L" not a numeric digit "1.")

Similarly, we represent the first difference of a variable, $Appr_t$, as $\Delta Y_t = Y_t - Y_{t-1}$. So ΔY_t is simply the period-to-period change in the level of Y. In Stata, the difference of a variable like "*Appr*" is computed in the following way:

```
d.Appr
```

Note that using the difference operator normally causes us to lose a case from our analysis because, according to the formula, we don't have a lagged value that pre-dates our first observation. In the example for the "*Appr*" variable, that is, there is no value for $\Delta Appr$ for January of 1993 because we do not have a value for "*Appr*" for President Clinton in December of 1992.[5]

12.3.3   Performing Time-Series Regression Analyses in Stata

Now that you know how to create time-series variables with lags and first differences, performing time-series regression analyses in Stata is just as simple as all of the other regression analyses you already know in Stata.

The data set that you should have open contains several other variables in addition to President Clinton's approval rating (the "*Appr*" variable). Of particular interest are three measures of consumer confidence, akin to what is described in Section 12.4 of the main text. The variable *ICS* is the Index of Consumer Sentiment, produced by the University of Michigan.[6] The five components of the *ICS* include measures of the public's views of both the past and the future of the economy, as it pertains both to a person's own financial situation and also to the economy as a whole. The index also includes an item about whether or not now is a good time to make major household purchases. Two of the components of the index are included in that data set: the variable *Pocket* assesses the public's beliefs about how their personal financial situation compares today to that of a year ago.[7] And the variable *BusFut* measures the public's perceptions of whether business conditions in the country are likely to get better or worse in the next five years.[8]

If we were to run a Koyck regression model on the relationship between President Clinton's approval rating and the overall Index of Consumer Sentiment, as presented in Section 12.3.5 of the main text, it would be of the form

$$Appr_t = \lambda Appr_{t-1} + \alpha + \beta_0 ICS_t + v_t.$$

---

[5] And getting such a value is impossible, because he was not President in December of 1992; George H.W. Bush was.

[6] Michigan's Survey of Consumers web site is: www.sca.isr.umich.edu/.

[7] The exact question wording is: "Would you say that you (and your family living there) are better off or worse off financially than you were a year ago?" Response options are "better," "same," or "worse."

[8] The exact question wording is: "Looking ahead, which would you say is more likely? That in the country as a whole we'll have continuous good times during the next five years or so, or that we'll have periods of widespread unemployment or depression, or what?" The response options are "good times," "uncertain," or "bad times."

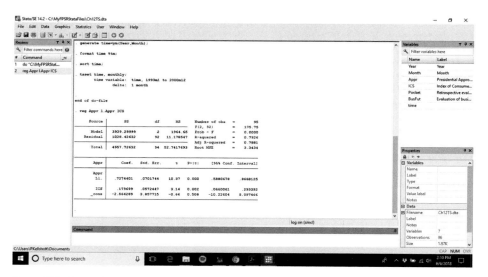

Figure 12.9: Output from a Koyck model in Stata

And in Stata, that would simply be the command:

```
reg Appr l.Appr ICS
```

The results of that command are presented in Figure 12.9.

Recall from Section 12.3.5 what each of the estimated coefficients represents. As you can see in the output in Figure 12.9, the coefficient of 0.179699 by the variable *ICS* represents the *immediate* impact of a one-point shift in the ICS on President Clinton's approval rating. When consumer confidence improves by one point, that is associated with an increase in President Clinton's approval of about 0.18 points. In other words, it would take a shift of a bit more than five points in consumer confidence to translate into a one-point shift in approval.

Perhaps that effect seems a bit small to you, but remember, the 0.18 only represents the *immediate* impact of a shift in consumer confidence on approval. The Koyck model allows us to compute the *cumulative* impact, β, of a one-point shift in the independent variable using the formula

$$\beta = \frac{\beta_0}{1 - \alpha}.$$

In this case, because $\alpha = 0.7274401$, this means that roughly 73% of a shift in the independent variable persists into the next period. Inserting this into the formula, we see that

$$\beta = \frac{0.179699}{1 - 0.7274401} = \frac{0.179699}{0.2725599} = 0.659301.$$

The Koyck model, you recall, explicitly models the idea that shifts in the independent variable at time t might take a while – multiple periods of time – to realize their full effect. In other words, a shift in consumer confidence in March might take part of April or even May (or beyond) to fully be translated into an approval rating. This means that the *cumulative* – that is, added up over time – effect of a one-point shift in consumer confidence is roughly two-thirds of a point of approval. That's a good bit bigger than its immediate impact, as you can see.

We remind you of the lesson from Section 12.3.5 that the value of the coefficient for the lagged dependent variable – which represents the way that lagged values of the *independent* variable continue to have lingering effects on the dependent variable – should vary between 0 and 1. If the value is 0, then there are no lagged effects of the independent variable on the dependent variable, and the cumulative effect is simply the immediate impact. (You can see this from the algebra of the formula.) But the closer the value of the coefficient for the lagged dependent variable gets to 1, the more the quotient for the cumulative effect will grow.[9]

12.4 EXERCISES

1. Open Stata and load the do-file named "Chapter 12 Multiple Regression Examples.do" into the do-file editor. Make sure that you have the correct directory path for loading the data. In other words, if "C:\MyFPSRStataFiles" is not where you have your data, change this part of the do-file so that the data load into Stata. Once you have done this, run the code to produce the results presented in Table 12.2 of *FPSR*. Copy and paste this figure into your word processing document.

2. Using the code at the bottom of "Chapter 12 Multiple Regression Examples.do" create a classification table for the BNL and the BNP models. Copy and paste this out into your word processing document.

3. Calculate the proportionate reduction in error from a naive model to the BNL and from a naive model to the BNP. Write briefly about what you have learned from doing this.

4. Using the data set Ch12TS.dta and the do-file Ch12TS.do, estimate a regression model of the effects of *ICS* on *Appr*, without using a lagged dependent variable in the model. Answer the following questions:

    (a) What does the output tell you about the effects of a one-point shift in consumer confidence on President Clinton's approval ratings?

    (b) Examining the Stata output, how well does the model fit the data? Point to specific parts of the output that help you arrive at your conclusion.

    (c) Time-series analysts refer to a bivariate model like this as a "static" regression. Can you guess why? In other words, does this model capture the lingering effects that consumer confidence might have in future months of approval? Is this a big problem or a small problem?

5. Using the data set Ch12TS.dta and the do-file Ch12TS.do, estimate a Koyck model of the effects of *ICS* on *Appr* as in Figure 12.9 – that is, including a lagged dependent variable in the model. Answer the following questions:

---

[9] Recall our admonition from the main text that if the coefficient for the lagged dependent variable equals or exceeds 1.0, this represents serious problems for our model.

(a)   What does the output tell you about the cumulative effects of a one-point shift in consumer confidence on President Clinton's approval ratings? How does this compare to the effects estimated in the previous question?

(b)   Examining the Stata output, how well does the model fit the data? Point to specific parts of the output that help you arrive at your conclusion. How do these model fit statistics compare to the fit statistics in the previous question?

(c)   What concerns might you still have about the model you just estimated?

6.   Using the data set Ch12TS.dta and the do-file Ch12TS.do, estimate a regression model of the effects of ΔICS on $\Delta Appr$ – that is, a model in first differences. Answer the following questions:

(a)   What does the output tell you about the effects of month-to-month changes in consumer confidence on month-to-month changes in President Clinton's approval ratings? How does this compare to the effects estimated in the previous two questions?

(b)   Examining the Stata output, how well does the model fit the data? Point to specific parts of the output that help you arrive at your conclusion. How do these model fit statistics compare to the fit statistics in the previous two questions? Does this make these models better or worse than the ones in previous questions?

(c)   If you were to include a lagged dependent variable in this model, what would that coefficient represent? (Choose your words very precisely!)

7.   Using the data set Ch12TS.dta and the do-file Ch12TS.do, estimate two separate Koyck models of the effects of *Pocket* and *BusFut* on *Appr*. Answer the following questions:

(a)   What does the output tell you about the effects of each of these components of consumer confidence on President Clinton's approval ratings? How do these results compare to the results for the overall ICS?

(b)   Now estimate a model that includes *both Pocket* and *BusFut*. How do these results compare to those just above? What might explain those differences?

(c)   How highly correlated are *Pocket* and *BusFut*? Why might this be relevant?

BIBLIOGRAPHY

Bansak, Kirk, Jens Hainmueller and Dominik Hangartner. 2016. "How economic, humanitarian, and religious concerns shape European attitudes toward asylum seekers." *Science* 354(6309): aag2147.

De Mesquita, Bruce Bueno, James D. Morrow, Randolph M. Siverson and Alastair Smith. 1999. "An institutional explanation of the democratic peace." *American Political Science Review* 93(4): 791–807.

Fair, Ray C. 1978. "The effect of economic events on votes for president." *Review of Economics and Statistics* 60: 159–173.

Fortunato, David, Randolph T. Stevenson and Greg Vonnahme. 2016. "Context and political knowledge: Explaining cross-national variation in partisan left–right knowledge." *Journal of Politics* 78(4): 1211–1228.

Heberlig, Eric, Marc Hetherington and Bruce Larson. 2006. "The price of leadership: Campaign money and the polarization of congressional parties." *Journal of Politics* 68(4): 992–1005.

King, Gary, Benjamin Schneer and Ariel White. 2017. "How the news media activate public expression and influence national agendas." *Science* 358(6364): 776–780.

Lipsmeyer, Christine S. and Heather Nicole Pierce. 2011. "The eyes that bind: Junior ministers as oversight mechanisms in coalition governments." *Journal of Politics* 73(4): 1152–1164.

O'Brien, Diana Z. 2015. "Rising to the top: Gender, political performance, and party leadership in parliamentary democracies." *American Journal of Political Science* 59(4): 1022–1039.

Stasavage, David. 2005. "Democracy and education spending in Africa." *American Journal of Political Science* 49(2): 343–358.

Titiunik, Rocio. 2016. "Drawing your senator from a jar: Term length and legislative behavior." *Political Science Research and Methods* 4(2): 293–316.

INDEX

Stata commands are emboldened.